Why Bad Presentations
Happen to
Good Causes

AND HOW TO ENSURE THEY
WON'T HAPPEN TO YOURS.

Written, Designed and Published by
ANDY GOODMAN & CAUSE COMMUNICATIONS
Creators of Why Bad Ads Happen to Good Causes

This book is dedicated to Anita S. Goodman,
who always taught her children to present themselves well.

TABLE OF CONTENTS

ACKNOWLEDGEMENTS

This book would not have been possible without the support and cooperation of the following individuals and organizations:

- The California Endowment, The California Wellness Foundation, The Edna McConnell Clark Foundation, The Harbourton Foundation, The William and Flora Hewlett Foundation, The Robert Wood Johnson Foundation, Open Society Institute, The David and Lucile Packard Foundation, The Sisters of Charity Foundation of Cleveland, and Surdna Foundation. Special thanks to Dennis Hunt, Magdalena Beltrán-del Olmo, Michael Bailin, Nancy Roob, Bruce Trachtenberg, Eric Brown, Amy Regan, David Morse, Gara LaMarche, Maria Teresa Rojas, Stephanie McAuliffe, Chris DeCardy, Susanna Krey, Julie Rittenhouse, and Vince Stehle.

- Chris Hershey, Andrew Posey, and Joanna Lee – the management and design team at Cause Communications – who have been my partners in this project since its inception. (Now we have two "bad" books behind us!)

- Pam Loeb, who helped design the survey and provided incisive analysis of the results; and Edge Research, which hosted the survey online.

- Our 20 expert commentators, who generously shared their time and insights: Cliff Atkinson, Max Atkinson, Joel Bradshaw, Geoffrey Canada, Marc Freedman, Dynell Garron, Kristen Grimm, Paul Hawken, Kim Klein, Christina Harbridge Law, Andy Lipkis, Chuck Loring, Nancy Lublin, Holly Minch, Lorraine Monroe, Peg Neuhauser, Eda Roth, Gerry Tabio, Scott Ward, and Jerry Weissman.

- Lindsey Pollak, who tracked down and interviewed most of our expert commentators, and managed to elicit a wealth of useful advice in the process.

- The Edna McConnell Clark Foundation, Environmental Defense, Nurse-Family Partnership, and Roca for allowing us to critique their PowerPoint presentations.

- The peer reviewers who patiently combed through early drafts of this book and helped make it both a stronger resource and a better read: Parker Blackman, Lisa Brei, Eric Brown, Roberto Cremonini, Chris DeCardy, John Gomperts, Kristen Grimm, Chris Hershey, Dennis Hunt, Brett Jenks, Pam Loeb, Jeff Martin, Terrence McNally, Holly Minch, David Morse, George Perlov, Lindsey Pollak, Amy Regan, Julie Rittenhouse, Maria Teresa Rojas, Vince Stehle, Bruce Trachtenberg, and Stefanie Weiss.

- Bud Pollak, who graciously gave up at least one full round of golf to edit this book.

- The individuals and organizations – too numerous to list here – who promoted our online survey and helped round up public interest professionals working across a wide range of issues in every region of the United States.

- The 2,501 respondents to the questionnaire who generously gave their time and candidly shared their experiences to provide unprecedented data about public interest presentations.

And most of all, I would like to thank Carolyn, Dan, and Olivia, who often make me wonder why such good people have happened to me.

Andy Goodman
January 2006

OVERVIEW

SUCH GOOD CAUSES, SUCH BAD PRESENTATIONS

How far back must you search in your memory to recall the last presentation that wasted your time? A week? A day? *An hour?* Rest assured: Your misery has plenty of company. Buttonhole any colleague who has been to an off-site or conference recently and you are bound to get an earful about endless data dumps, bullet-riddled PowerPoint, lifeless speakers, and rooms colder than meat lockers. Who among us has escaped the sinking feeling that follows those dreaded words, "I just have a few more slides"?

For the last five years, I have been traveling around the country, delivering speeches and conducting workshops exclusively for nonprofits, foundations, educational institutions and government agencies. In doing so, I have learned what it takes to engage, inform, and motivate an audience of public interest professionals. And by watching dozens of other presentations (while awaiting my turn or just session-hopping at conferences), I have also learned that Albert Einstein was right: Time *can* slow down. In fact, I have witnessed presentations where it has stopped entirely.

Which led me to wonder: Why are so many of our colleagues – decent, well-educated, well-intentioned folks – so good at being so boring? Has their devotion to data and sound science made them forget that audiences need not only to be educated, but emotionally engaged as well? Are they so imbued with the righteousness of their causes that they do not feel obligated to be interesting? Are they just too damn smart for their own good?

To be fair, good causes are not the only entities bedeviled by bad presentations. But from where I have been sitting (and sitting, and sitting) it appears our sector is boldly pioneering new frontiers of badness. In the fall of 2004, driven by curiosity and the fear that "bored to death" was more than just an expression, I decided to find out why.

HAD THE STORIES. NEEDED THE NUMBERS.

When I talk to audiences about storytelling, I always remind them that telling stories is not enough to make your case. Stories are a terrific way to bring large issues down to ground level where people can get their minds (and hearts) around them. But after you have told your story, you must back it up with the numbers that prove you have more than one story to tell.

To answer the question posed by this book's title, I knew we did not need to dwell on the stories. Everybody I met had at least one. So I immediately started searching for any existing research that could objectively quantify the factors that make presentations in our sector succeed or fail. When I set out to write *Why Bad Ads Happen to Good Causes*, I had Roper Starch's database and 10 years' worth of public interest advertisements to draw from. For this book, though, there was nothing even remotely comparable. I had to start fresh.

Chris Hershey, president of Cause Communications, and my partner in producing *Bad Ads*, worked with me to design a questionnaire that would prompt candid comments about the good, bad, and (mostly) ugly of public interest presentations. In January 2005, we posted it on the web, where it was hosted by Edge Research, the company that would oversee the quantitative research and help us analyze the results. We worked our networks to publicize the survey, and within three months, 2,501 public interest professionals had visited Edge's site and completed the online questionnaire. *(For a complete description of the survey methodology, please refer to the Appendix.)*

Now Add the Best and the Brightest

While crunching the numbers produced by the survey, we also conducted some qualitative research. One of our survey questions asked, "Who are the best presenters you have seen in the past year or two?" As you might expect when over 2,000 people respond, this question produced a long list of names. Several names were repeated so often, however, that we felt reasonably certain the survey had identified many of the leading lights in our field. We contacted these individuals and asked them to share their insights into the art of presenting.

We also interviewed the authors of some of the best-known books on presenting, as well as highly regarded public speaking coaches who have conducted trainings in our sector. As a result, in addition to my experience and the data from our survey, *Why Bad Presentations Happen to Good Causes* also draws from the expertise of the following 20 talented men and women:

- **Cliff Atkinson**, President, Sociable Media (Los Angeles, CA)
- **Max Atkinson,** President, Atkinson Communications (Wells, Somerset, U.K.)
- **Joel Bradshaw,** President, Joel Bradshaw Associates (Falls Church, VA)
- **Geoffrey Canada,** President & CEO, Harlem Children's Zone (New York, NY)
- **Marc Freedman,** Founder & President, Civic Ventures (San Francisco, CA)
- **Dynell Garron,** Founder, The Funder's Checklist (Oakland, CA)
- **Kristen Grimm,** President, Spitfire Strategies (Washington, DC)
- **Paul Hawken,** Founder, Natural Capital Institute (Sausalito, CA)
- **Kim Klein,** Founder & Publisher, *Grassroots Fundraising Journal* (Oakland, CA)
- **Christina Harbridge Law,** President, Bridgeport Financial, Inc. (San Francisco, CA)
- **Andy Lipkis,** Founder & President, TreePeople (Beverly Hills, CA)
- **Chuck V. Loring,** CFRE, Senior Partner, Loring, Sternberg & Associates (Ft. Lauderdale, FL)
- **Nancy Lublin,** CEO, Do Something (New York, NY)
- **Holly Minch,** Project Director, SPIN Project (San Francisco, CA)

- **Lorraine Monroe,** President & CEO, Lorraine Monroe Leadership Institute (New York, NY)
- **Peg Neuhauser,** President, PCN Associates (Austin, TX)
- **Eda Roth,** Eda Roth & Associates (Boston, MA)
- **Gerry Tabio,** President, Creative Resources (Bixby, OK)
- **Scott Ward,** Senior Vice President, Widmeyer Communications (Washington, DC)
- **Jerry Weissman,** Founder, Power Presentations, Ltd. (Foster City, CA)

(A brief biography of each expert commentator appears in the Appendix.)

Last but not least, I reviewed numerous books, magazine and newspaper articles, and combed through web sites that dealt with presenting or public speaking to find further examples of best practices or common pitfalls. (The best of these publications are listed in the Resources section at the back of this book.) Insights from this research were also considered as we used the survey results and our experts' advice to develop the recommendations that appear in this book.

WHAT YOU WILL FIND INSIDE

Chapter 1, "The Sorry State of the Art," summarizes the top-line results from our unprecedented research and explains why the average public interest presentation earns a below-average grade (C-minus, to be exact). This chapter identifies the problems that most often sabotage presentations ("The Fatal Five"), the qualities audiences find most desirable ("The Three Most Wanted"), and suggests three reasons why bad presentations happen to good causes.

As we anticipated, there is much more to be found wanting in public interest presentations than there is to be admired, but the news is not entirely discouraging. The chapter concludes with "Five Glimmers of Hope," indications from our survey that presenters want to improve in precisely the areas where the most improvement is needed.

That rehabilitation will begin, hopefully, with the following chapter, "Building Better Presentations." Even when you have truly compelling information to share, if you do not consider your audience's level of interest, ability to absorb information, inclination to interact, and other factors, you may find your talk falling on deaf ears. Chapter 2 will help you design more informative, engaging, and persuasive presentations by keeping your focus where it belongs – on your audience – from the first moment you begin planning your talk to the last word that comes out of your mouth.

With all the required parts of your presentation in place, you will be ready to consider how you, the presenter, can energize your material and keep your audience fully engaged. Chapter 3, "Improving Your Delivery," covers basic platform skills that can help you use your eyes, voice and body to deliver your message with more authority, ensure that key points are conveyed, and sustain audience interest from start to finish.

The last two chapters drill down into the nitty-gritty of presenting. According to our survey, over 60% of public interest professionals use visuals to support their presentations, and in most cases that means PowerPoint. Chapter 4, "PowerPoint Is Your Friend," offers seven recommendations for making the most of this ubiquitous but much maligned software. And Chapter 5, "The Small Stuff (It's Worth Sweating)" offers tips on preparing handouts, creating evaluation forms, securing the right equipment, and nailing down all those other details nobody notices … until something goes wrong.

By the time you reach the back of this book, you may feel like you have been given more guidelines, recommendations, and to-do lists than one person can reasonably hope to remember. So, we have summarized the most essential take-away in checklists that are designed, literally, to be taken away. Look for them in the Resources section under "Checklists to Go" and just cut along the dotted lines.

So, Is This Book for You?

When Cause Communications and I first discussed plans for this book, we loosely defined our audience as any public interest professional who has to speak to more than five people for more than five minutes on a previously assigned topic. Through our research, however, we have developed a clearer picture of the kinds of individuals who can benefit from reading this book.

In our survey, we asked respondents to describe the presentations they give and to evaluate their own levels of skill. By doing so, what we initially viewed as an undifferentiated mass of good-hearted, hard-working people divided itself into five categories of presenters:

All-Stars (18% of survey respondents): This group excels at all aspects of presenting, from developing an initial outline to performing at the podium. This is no accident: While All-Stars may have some natural gifts, they have invested in formal training or read relevant publications (or both) to hone their skills. All-Stars are inclined to seek feedback from others, but they do not rehearse as often as other kinds of presenters, most likely because they do not feel the need. All-Stars tend to use visuals such as PowerPoint and regularly bring handouts for audience members. Not only do they interact with their audience in the course of a typical presentation, they are the only group who consistently encourages audience members to interact with one another. Of the five groups, they are most confident in their skills and genuinely look forward to opportunities to present.

Naturals (20%): In basic skill level, this group resembles the All-Stars. They follow most of the principles that define good presentations, but this is a result more of intuition than formal training or independent study. Naturals spend more time rehearsing than All-Stars, but not as much as some of the groups below. While they are comfortable interacting with their audiences and do so consistently, they rarely encourage peer-to-peer interaction between audience members.

The Unplugged (17%): At first glance, this third cluster resembles both the All-Stars and Naturals, but there is a key difference: The Unplugged generally work without visual materials (most notably PowerPoint) when they present. While many in this group have had more formal training than the Naturals, they are less likely to seek feedback after a presentation is over.

Draftees (23%): The largest of the five categories, this group could also be called "The Coalition of the Unwilling." Draftees present because they have to. They have had little formal training to hone their skills and haven't read much about presenting on their own. They do not spend a lot of time preparing in advance or soliciting feedback once a presentation has been completed. Draftees tend to give themselves fair to good ratings, but their feelings about presenting are lukewarm compared to the groups described above.

Jitterbugs (17%): Members of this group have had little or no formal training and haven't studied presenting on their own. They know what they don't know, but being honest with themselves doesn't make them any more confident. To compensate, Jitterbugs are most likely to spend ample time rehearsing before they present, but this may only mean refining bad habits or getting more comfortable delivering bad content. They tend to shy away from any type of audience interaction. Lacking confidence in their ability to present, Jitterbugs dread getting up in front of just about any group, large or small.

Does one of these categories describe you? What they say to us very clearly is that roughly four out of five public interest professionals who present could, by their own admission, use some help. Cause Communications and I developed *Why Bad Presentations Happen to Good Causes* to provide that help, but our ultimate objective is not simply to help you design spiffier slides or learn the right way to make eye contact.

We recognize that you do important work, often with limited resources and against long odds. Every time you talk about that work, you have an opportunity to inspire people who can help you in some way. This book is about seeing those opportunities for what they are, taking full advantage of them, and setting a new standard across our sector where our presentations are consistently as good as our causes.

Please note: survey respondents who did not answer certain questions could not be included in the "cluster analysis" that allowed us to identify the five categories of presenters described above. As a result, these categories add up to 95% instead of 100%.

Chapter 1:

The Sorry State of the Art

*Why the Average Presentation
Earns a Below-Average Grade*

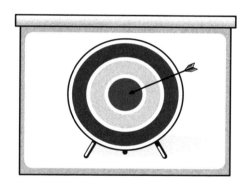

"The human brain starts working
the moment you are born and
never stops until you stand up to
speak in public."

– ANONYMOUS

The word "presentation" can mean different things to different people. When we first began designing our survey, we consulted with colleagues who asked questions such as, "Are you including an impromptu five-minute talk at a staff meeting?" "Are speeches presentations?" "What about day-long workshops?"

We wanted to keep the definition fairly broad in order to help a wide range of presenters, so we used the first few questions in our survey to let respondents set the parameters themselves. For better or worse, here are the specifications they provided for the average public interest presentation:

THE AVERAGE PRESENTATION DEFINED

LENGTH	10–60 minutes *(with most running approx. 20 minutes)*
AUDIENCE SIZE	10–50 people
USE OF VISUALS	62% of presentations use visuals of some sort, with PowerPoint being the visual application of choice.
USE OF HANDOUTS	60% of presenters provide handouts to their audience.
INTERACTION BETWEEN SPEAKER & AUDIENCE	24% of presentations feature interaction between speaker and audience beyond traditional Q&A *(e.g., speaker circulates among audience during breakouts).*
INTERACTION BETWEEN AUDIENCE MEMBERS	8% of presenters ask audience members to interact with each other in the course of a presentation.

Of particular note here are the exceptionally low percentages reported for the last two categories. As you will see in the results that follow, **audience members want to interact with the people in the room.** They appreciate opportunities to draw upon the expertise of presenters (beyond what the typical question-and-answer session offers), but they see such opportunities as rare. They also consider their fellow audience members to be potential resources, but opportunities to interact with them are viewed as even fewer and farther between.

Even though these first few questions were intended to elicit a neutral picture of the average presentation, the responses were already pointing up areas of deficiency. And that, as they say, was just for starters.

COMMON PROBLEMS: THE FATAL FIVE

After covering the basic specifications (and getting more than we bargained for), we asked respondents to evaluate several factors that can derail a presentation. We also gave them the opportunity to suggest factors that may not have been listed in the survey. The results were not surprising. Like teachers dissatisfied with their students' work, the respondents handed out one bad grade after another:

- The average grade public interest professionals gave to the presentations they attended was C– (i.e., average score of 2.9 on a scale of 1 to 5).
- The average grade given to the visuals (most commonly PowerPoint) that respondents observed in presentations they attended was also C–.
- The average grade given to handouts respondents received during or after presentations they attended was C.
- When asked to recall presentations they had seen over the last few months, survey respondents said they were more than twice as likely (54% vs. 25%) to see a poor presentation as an excellent one.

As we analyzed the responses to both closed-ended and open-ended questions, we were able to identify five factors as the most problematic for presentations. The "Fatal Five" are:

1. **Reading the slides.** More respondents complained about this behavior than anything else – and by a wide margin. Many indignantly asked why a presenter would read slides aloud when audience members were entirely capable of reading them for themselves. Several others pointed out that not only did they have slides read to them, the text of those slides was on handouts they had already received. (In presenting lingo, this is referred to as the dreaded "triple play," i.e., the same text is on the screen, read aloud, and in a handout.) "Watching someone read PowerPoint slides is a form of torture that should be banned under the Geneva Convention," wrote one respondent.

2. **Too long, too much information.** How long is too long? If a presentation is boring, respondents told us, even 10 minutes can seem too long. And boring presentations appear to be rampant across the sector. On far too many occasions, said those surveyed, presentations feel like unedited downloads of information that they must sift through on their own to find relevance and practical application. "Too much of everything," answered one respondent when we asked what makes a poor presentation. "Too many slides with too many words, too many points, too much data, too long, too didactic."

3. **Lack of interaction.** The problem that first appeared when we asked respondents to describe the typical presentation resurfaced strongly in subsequent answers to open-ended questions. Many complained about being "talked at" for 30, 40, even 60 minutes at a time. "[The] straight lecture format is boring and puts me right to sleep. I need Q&A or the chance for the audience to leap in there in more of a discussion-style format," wrote one respondent. Several others commented on the frequently missed opportunity to learn from their peers. "Presenters often forget that many in the audience, particularly those, say, from 35 and up, have life and work experience that is

> *"People go to nonprofit conferences to learn something to make their organization better. I've sat through a lot of workshops and I've thought, two days from now, will people have any ideas they can actually put into effect? That may be the biggest failing."*
>
> – CHUCK LORING
> LORING, STERNBERG
> & ASSOCIATES

waiting to be shared," wrote another respondent. "Presenters have a responsibility to mine that, direct it, and facilitate the economical sharing of that information among the group."

4. **Lifeless presenters.** Presenters who speak in a monotone, who seem to lack interest in their own material, or who appear to have wandered in from the set of "Night of the Living Dead" were also reported by many in the survey. "Even if I'm interested in the topic," one respondent told us, "if the speaker is boring, I'm easily distracted by other goings-on in the room like someone's cool shoes or outfit. And then I'm totally lost thinking, 'I need to go shopping!'"

5. **Room/technical problems.** LCD projectors that don't work, air conditioning that works too well, sound systems that are either too soft, too loud, or have too much hiss – just about every room or technical problem you can imagine showed up in survey answers. While equipment breakdowns and room problems are inevitable across thousands of presentations, many are preventable, and even those that cannot be avoided do not have to ruin a talk. The frequency with which respondents mentioned these kinds of problems suggests that public interest presenters often do not anticipate them or fail to have a backup plan.

> "When I go to most presentations, I want to die. They're just reading to me. Give me something to do. Make this an experience I'll remember. We don't learn from facts and figures. We learn by doing. The whole point of that human being up on the platform is to create an experience."
>
> – CHRISTINA HARBRIDGE LAW
> BRIDGEPORT FINANCIAL, INC.

EXCELLENCE DEFINED: THE THREE MOST WANTED

In another open-ended question, we asked, "What one or two key things make a presentation excellent?" Again, respondents provided a wide range of answers, although a few unhappy campers claimed they had *never* seen an excellent presentation. A consensus emerged around three characteristics, and unsurprisingly each is a direct opposite of a common problem cited above.

1. **Interaction.** Nearly one out of every four respondents mentioned interaction – with the speaker, with other audience members, or both – as a hallmark of excellent presentations. "Interactive presentations that create opportunities for the audience members to work together and with the presenter are almost always top notch," one respondent told us.

2. **Clarity.** Some used the words "well organized," and some wrote "concise," but if you were to scan the verbatim responses to this question, you would see a long run of answers that begin with "clarity." One such response: "Clarity of three to four well-framed key points the speaker wanted the audience to take away, coupled with smart use of metaphors/anecdotes that helped speaker drive them home."

3. **Enthusiasm.** Whether respondents used the words energy, passion, charisma, engaging, dynamic or lively, they all wanted the same thing: presenters who were enthusiastic about their topic and conveyed that interest to the audience.

Four other qualities that each received a high number of mentions were: humor, use of stories, relevance, and well-produced visuals.

THE LINK BETWEEN EXCELLENCE AND LEARNING

The survey also revealed one other characteristic of excellent presentations that was not so easily anticipated. When we asked respondents how often they felt they learned something valuable from a typical presentation, roughly a third (34%) said "usually" or "always." Note in the list below, though, how this number increases as specific elements of the presentation improve from average to good:

Respondents who say they "usually" or "always" learn something valuable

… from the average presentation: 34%

… from presentations where audience members interact with the speaker: 47%

… from presentations where audience members interact with each other: 53%

… from presentations with "good handouts": 54%

… from presentations with "good visuals": 57%

These numbers suggest that excellence is worth pursuing not only for its own sake, but because audience members clearly believe they learn more from better presentations.

WHY DO BAD PRESENTATIONS HAPPEN TO GOOD CAUSES?

By asking respondents to comment on presentations they had seen, we were able to obtain a clearer picture of what was going wrong in our sector. The survey's next set of questions, in which respondents evaluated their own presentations, was designed to probe a deeper question: **Why** is our sector producing so many bad presentations? We believe there are three reasons:

1. MOST PUBLIC INTEREST PROFESSIONALS "PREPARE TO FAIL."

Before going any further, it is worth considering the different kinds of expertise that comprise the skill of presenting, especially for those skeptics who may still consider it a necessary evil and little more. There are reasons why professional presenters command large speaking fees:

First, skilled presenters know how to take raw information and manipulate it into a package that can fit a given time frame while still ensuring that the audience will absorb and understand the major points.

Second, unless they have someone helping them prepare, skilled presenters create their own slides, overheads, charts or other supporting visuals that can help the audience absorb the material more readily. And when they work *without* visuals, they know how to craft a speech that can hold the audience's attention on its own merits.

And finally, skilled presenters know how to present, which means engaging a room full of people who may be distracted, addicted to their BlackBerrys, only vaguely interested in the topic, downright hostile, or all of the above. They have learned enough about the audience in advance to tailor their comments to the people in the room, and they have developed their "platform skills" to the point where they are completely comfortable at the podium, no matter how many pairs of eyes are staring at them.

Acquiring all these skills takes time, and even highly skilled presenters know that when they must develop an entirely new presentation, they are in for hours upon hours of work. Synthesizing reams of information into a few understandable and easily memorized points can take several hours if not days. Creating slides or other graphics that support the presenter (as opposed to simply duplicating his content) takes more time. And getting to a comfort level with the material where the presenter can focus on the audience (and whether or not they are "getting it") instead of trying to remember the next point – that can take hours of rehearsal or even several actual presentations (assuming the talk will be given more than once).

Now consider how respondents to our survey answered the following questions about the amount of work they put into their presentations:

How much time, on average, do you spend preparing for a presentation?	More than half (53%) spend a grand total of 2 hours or less.
How often do you rehearse for a presentation, either alone or for a test audience?	Less than half (45%) say they "always" or "usually" rehearse, and 35% report rehearsing rarely or never.
How much formal training have you had to improve your presentation skills?	Only 10% say they have had a "significant amount" of training.
How many publications have you read to help improve your presentation skills?	Only 6% say they have read a "significant number" of publications.

2. IN A WORD: DENIAL.

In one section of our survey, we asked respondents to rate the visuals, handouts, and other aspects of presentations they had *given*. In another section we asked them to rate the same list of elements in presentations they had *attended*.

By comparing those responses side by side (as in the chart below), it became apparent that respondents are much harsher critics of other people's presentations than they are of their own:

How often would you rate these elements as "good-to-excellent" in presentations ...	You Give?	You See?
VISUALS	46%	19%
HANDOUTS	64%	24%
INTERACTION (SPEAKER W/AUDIENCE)	64%	24%
INTERACTION (AMONG AUDIENCE MEMBERS)	24%	8%
ALL ELEMENTS COMBINED (I.E., OVERALL PRESENTATION)	49%	18%

So, do these numbers simply illustrate a sector-wide case of "I'm Okay, You Stink" Syndrome, or do they tell us something more? I believe they do, especially the final comparison.

Take a closer look: 82% of respondents told us they were **not** seeing good-to-excellent presentations. At the same time, 49% claimed to be delivering good-to-excellent presentations. Which raises the question: *delivering to whom?* Is it possible that their presentations were as good as they claimed, and that all those bad presentations respondents saw were delivered by people *outside* the survey?

Anything is possible. It just does not seem very likely. What appears far more likely is that a certain river associated with Egypt has cut a wide swath through our sector, and that many public interest presenters have yet to face the truth: Their presentations are not as good as they think.

3. Expectations continue to *lower* the bar.

When bad presentations are as commonplace as they are across the public interest sector, suffering through one is hardly noteworthy. We enter the meeting rooms, have our pants bored off us for any number of hours, and then leave in search of coffee, cookies, or a ride home. We may be bored, but we're not particularly upset. When was the last time you saw someone buttonholing a conference organizer to demand higher quality presentations?

To a certain extent, this problem is exacerbated by human nature. "People imitate what they see," says Christina Harbridge Law, a presentation coach. "If we see someone read PowerPoint, we'll do it. It takes courage to stand out and do it differently." With a dearth of good models, we continue to emulate mediocrity and worse.

And then there is the problem of conference organizers whose expectations are not only low, but wrong-headed. At one national health conference, for example, I was asked to submit my PowerPoint presentation in advance so it could be translated into print and distributed to conference attendees prior to my talk. The thinking behind this practice, which is not uncommon, is that printed copies of the slides (1) help audience members take notes more easily, and (2) provide a summary of the presentation for conferees who cannot attend the talk. And this thinking was so deeply entrenched, in fact, that all speakers invited to this conference were *required* to submit their presentations in advance.

I refused to comply for several reasons. First, as any experienced presenter will tell you, capturing and holding an audience's attention is always a challenge. People are easily distracted, and handouts received prior to a talk are pure fodder for distraction. The moment audience members get bored or confused, they will invariably start flipping through the handout to find something more interesting or to see what's coming up next. And now the presenter must work harder to regain their attention. So, why would I want to help them ignore me? (Handouts can, of course, play a valuable part in your presentation, but more on that in Chapter 5.)

Second, my PowerPoint presentation is designed to support my talk, not duplicate it. While some slides might make sense on their own, most are incomplete without my narration and would be confusing to anyone who missed the presentation. And finally, I like to use humor in my presentations, and some of my slides act like punch lines to jokes. Show me the comedian who hands out written copies of his punch lines in advance, and I'll show you someone who isn't working anymore.

Fortunately, the conference organizer who asked for my slides relented, but her grudging agreement "to make an exception" in my case only made me shake my head. At times, it looks to me as if public interest presenters are working in The Bizarro World, a planet where everything is backward and the people who request your presentation are bound and determined to help you ruin it.

FIVE GLIMMERS OF HOPE

While presenters may have an inflated sense of their own ability, and even if they are working in a climate that drags them down, there are reasons to believe improvement can come. The final open-ended question posed in our survey was, "As a presenter yourself, where do you see the most room for improvement?" The most frequent answers match up very well with the areas that need the most improvement. Specifically, respondents expressed the desire:

- *to find ways in which they can get audience members more involved;*
- *to learn how to better organize their material;*
- *to be more confident at the podium;*
- *to find more time to prepare for their presentations;*
- *to learn how to create more compelling visuals.*

In the following four chapters, we'll suggest specific ways to reach each of these goals.

CHAPTER 2:

BUILDING BETTER PRESENTATIONS

How to Take Your Audience from A to B

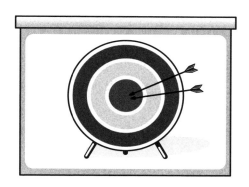

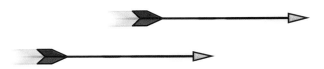

"Simplicity is the ultimate sophistication."

— Leonardo da Vinci

There are many different ways to structure a presentation, and if you attend seminars or read books on the subject, you will invariably encounter experts who tout their way as *the* way. In my opinion, the best structure is the one you are most comfortable with, and even that may change from one presentation to the next.

There may be times when a problem-solution format is best. On other occasions, a presentation that follows the arc of a story may be most appropriate. Or you may find yourself building a case like a courtroom lawyer. These are all reliable choices, but the important point here is that *you have to choose*. Presentations need structure just as tall buildings need steel frames. Otherwise, the whole thing can come crashing down on your head.

The following section outlines a basic structure that can serve you well for a variety of subjects. I encourage you to investigate other possibilities (the books in the Resources section offer several), but if you are like many of our survey respondents who seek a better way to organize their material, the framework below may be the best place to start.

THE AUDIENCE: START HERE

A common mistake in planning a presentation is asking yourself the seemingly innocent question, "What do I want to say?" Unfortunately, this places the initial focus on you and your material and not where it actually belongs: *on the audience*. Start with this question, and you are off on a path of building a case (or telling a story, or solving a problem) that may seem compelling to you, but may fall on deaf ears.

Joel Bradshaw, a veteran political strategist who frequently works with environmental organizations, has seen many clients make this mistake. "Most conservation organizations think that you persuade people by marshaling a series of scientific arguments and facts to change people's minds," says Bradshaw. "In reality, that isn't what happens. You change people's minds by figuring out what is important to them – which is rarely science – and you present arguments on *their* terms."

To keep your focus on the audience, as Bradshaw recommends, think of the presentation as their journey along the continuum below.

Where they are.   Where you want them to be.

See **Checklists to Go**
*for a detachable
summary of this section.*

A is what they are thinking and feeling when they enter the room. **B** is what you want them to think, feel, *and do* when they leave.

To move audience members along this path, you have to know something about them. This may require interviewing the conference organizer who scheduled your session. If you are working with a single organization, it may mean finding someone on the inside who can provide background on meeting attendees. Whatever the circumstances, there is almost always someone who will know more about the people in the room than you do. Find them, grill them, and take copious notes as they answer these questions:

Who will be in the audience?
One of the fastest ways to lose an audience is to begin talking above or below their level of knowledge or outside their job descriptions. Knowing job titles, having a general sense of the work they do, and learning as much as you can about their interest and understanding of your specific subject will help you pitch your talk at the appropriate level.

What do they know or believe that I can build on?
Rarely will you face an audience that is a blank slate. They are bound to have some feelings about your subject, and you want to fan whatever flickers of interest or support are out there. If you are proposing a plan for carpooling, for example, you may know going in that many people find it inconvenient and a hassle. But you are also likely to find that those same people hate sitting in traffic, and that will give you a better place to start.

What do they know or believe that I have to overcome?
Similarly, you don't want to walk into an ambush. If the room is filled with people who aren't sympathetic or even have reasons to oppose you, knowing this in advance will help you prepare arguments that speak directly to their concerns. When I talk to audiences about storytelling, for example, I often find that people are predisposed to think of stories as fun and entertaining, but certainly not a critical part of their communications toolkit. So I begin my presentations by naming that objection and helping audiences work past it. Only then can I move on to my goal, which is showing them how to use storytelling in their workplace.

By the end of my presentation, what do I want them to have learned?
In a typical one-hour presentation, the audience will only remember a handful of points. (More on this later.) So as you plan your talk, ask yourself: What three or four points would I want them to walk away with if they remembered nothing else?

By the end of my presentation, what do I want them to feel?
Human beings are emotional creatures by nature. If you present people with information without engaging their emotions in some way, the end result is often an audience that says, "That was interesting," and then promptly returns to their business and forgets everything you just told them. If you want your audience to be angry, hopeful, fed up, curious, or inspired, you have to build toward that emotion, so know in advance how you want to send them off.

By the end of my presentation, what do I want them to do?
Don't expect the audience to figure this part out for themselves. If you want them to consider your case, learn more, call their senator, march in the street, or whatever, you have to explicitly build that "ask" into your presentation.

Experienced speakers who give the same presentation many times regularly ask such questions in order to tailor their material to each new audience. "Tailoring is ALL," says Jerry Weissman, author of *Presenting to Win*. Before conducting a presentation training for her clients, Christina Harbridge Law asks them to complete a five-page questionnaire. Peg Neuhauser, who delivers about 100 presentations in a year, will conduct up to 30 interviews with a single client organization.

LENGTH: WHY MORE ISN'T NECESSARILY MORE

How long should it take to travel from A to B? Let me say definitively and without fear of contradiction: It depends.

When the Time for the Presentation is Fixed

At most meetings or conferences, formal presentations are allotted one hour. The common expectation among session planners is that this will be comprised of 45–50 minutes for the presentation and 10–15 minutes for a question-and-answer session at the end. (When the slot is 30 minutes, the breakdown is customarily 20–25 minutes for the presentation and 5–10 minutes for Q&A.)

If you believe that more time is required to cover your material in a manner that ensures real learning will occur, then you have two choices: (1) request more time, or (2) tailor your presentation to the time allowed and cover only the most important points. If this leaves the audience wanting more – which is a *good* thing – you can always provide a handout covering any points you did not have time to discuss, offer to stay after the session for additional Q&A, or provide your e-mail address to continue the conversation online. What you do *not* want to do, however, is jam all of your material into the time slot regardless of the fit.

While some presenters may think this approach gives audience members "more for their money," it actually does them a disservice. In his book *Multimedia Learning*, Richard Mayer analyzed how the amount of content in a presentation can affect an audience's ability to learn. "A concise presentation allows the learner … to focus on the key elements and mentally organize them in a way that makes sense," wrote Mayer. "In short … students tend to learn more when less is presented."

"How well we communicate is determined not by how well we say things, but by how well we are understood."

– ANDY GROVE
CO-FOUNDER, INTEL

There may also be occasions when you are allocated *more* time than you feel is necessary to adequately cover your subject. Under those circumstances, do not feel obliged to fill the time. "If [session organizers] ask for more than 1½ or two hours," says Peg Neuhauser, "I start asking why. I will argue with a long length – even though I can charge more – because it is just as important that everybody walk away happy." (In this vein, it is worth noting that of the 2,501 public interest professionals who completed our survey, not one complained about a presentation being too short.)

When the Time for the Presentation is Flexible

If the length is up to you, decide how long it will take to (a) cover your material, (b) engage your audience in learning exercises, and (c) send them off ready to act on what they have just learned or to employ the skill they have just acquired. When Gerry Tabio teaches creative problem solving, for example, he insists on a minimum of four hours. When I work with larger organizations (i.e., more than 100 staff members) on storytelling, I often request an entire day for the workshop.

Be advised, however, that when you plan a session of several hours, you have to break up the time. "I use roughly an hour as people's butt-in-one-place limit," says Chuck Loring, who speaks frequently on nonprofit governance. Kristen Grimm of Spitfire Strategies observes an even tighter schedule: "I don't talk for longer than 20 minutes *ever*, about anything. At that point, you get brain drift, and people need a break of some sort. I think of it as a cup you have filled, and people need to empty that cup before you can put more in."

A 1978 study of medical students' attention spans during one-hour lectures confirms Grimm's observation on "brain drift." The study, which was reported in *The Psychology of Teaching Methods* (University of Chicago Press, © 1976), tested over 1,300 students after they had attended 12 different lectures. By asking questions related to material covered at different times in each lecture, the study was able to determine how the students' attention rose and fell over the course of an hour. The conclusion: Attention rose steadily over the first 5–10 minutes, peaked around 15–20 minutes, and dropped sharply after that, never regaining the higher levels of those first few minutes.

In short: When the length is up to you, take as many hours as you need. But always remember that within any given hour, the audience has needs, too. For the remainder of this chapter, we will focus on the construction of a single hour, which will serve you equally well whether that hour represents your entire presentation or just one segment within a longer workshop.

Don't download – synthesize

"When you talk for an hour to a group, they are not going to remember the whole hour," says Kim Klein, who presents on fundraising as often as twice a week. "They'll probably only remember three things. So pick three things, illustrate them, and repeat them." This advice was echoed by many of our expert commentators, with most agreeing that the magic number of retainable main points was somewhere between three and five.

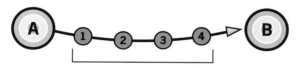

Identify the major points that make your case or explain your subject.

Once you decide which main points are essential to your presentation, sort through your materials to find the data, visuals, stories or other elements that will reinforce each point – *and put the rest aside*. Rather than add to your presentation, extraneous information and images only confuse and overburden the audience. So when in doubt, leave it out.

Peg Neuhauser tries to find a story to illustrate each point she wants to make, and she told us that if she cannot find a story, she is likely to drop the point. "The audience won't be convinced anyway," she says, "so why keep it in?"

In his book, *Lend Me Your Ears*, Max Atkinson describes a study he conducted that vividly shows the value of supporting each point with examples. By training one video camera on a speaker, a second on the audience, and putting both images side-by-side on a split-screen, Atkinson was able to precisely monitor how the audience members reacted throughout a presentation. The tapes showed that, "almost every time a speaker used the phrase 'for example,' people's heads or eyes would move upward in anticipation of what was to come."

> "If everything I want to present is a foot long, at the end they'll remember about an inch."
>
> – CHRISTINA HARBRIDGE LAW BRIDGEPORT FINANCIAL, INC.

KEEP IT INTERACTIVE

There are three good reasons to incorporate interactive segments into any presentation running more than 10 to 15 minutes:

First, your audience wants it. Of all the things we learned about public interest professionals through our survey, their desire to interact with the presenter and their colleagues in the room is strong and, unfortunately, usually unfulfilled. Addressing this desire alone would probably improve audience evaluations of your presentation by one full grade.

Second, it helps to break up the one-way flow of information. Attention spans are short, distractions are many, and most meeting rooms are not equipped with the most comfortable seats. (That may keep people awake, but it is no guarantee of attentiveness.) Human beings can only absorb so much information in a single, uninterrupted blast before they tune out, pass out, or start sending text messages to each other. Having people stand and stretch can get the blood flowing in their bodies, but a well-conceived interactive exercise can activate their minds as well.

Third, interactive exercises enhance learning. Too often, presenters approach their audience with what Richard Mayer calls "the empty vessel view of learning." The audience is the empty vessel, and all the presenter has to do is pour information into them for learning to transpire. If the audience were comprised of computers, that would work just fine. Human beings, on the other hand, need a little more love and care.

> "In the presentation room, I try not to talk for more than 10 to 15 minutes at a time. Then I give people a chance to digest and interact with the information. I talk through a concept quickly and then give people a chance to respond. That time frame forces you to keep things dynamic – like a conversation as opposed to a lecture."
>
> – HOLLY MINCH
> SPIN PROJECT

THE MAGIC NUMBER 7: NOT SO MAGICAL

Some experts may tell you with complete confidence that a presentation should contain around seven major points, or that an individual slide should contain no more than six bullets. As proof, they will refer to the paper, "The Magical Number Seven, Plus or Minus Two," published by George Miller.

In the 1950s, Miller conducted experiments to determine the number of units of information the average person can recall, and the answer is reflected in the paper's title. Over the years, though, the title has evolved into a rule that has been used to limit everything from the number of words on highway billboards to the amount of text on PowerPoint presentations.

Only it shouldn't be. When Miller conducted his tests, he did not expose subjects to *related* pieces of information as you would find in a presentation (or on a billboard, for that matter). Instead, he deliberately presented subjects with completely unrelated bits of information to see how many could be recalled given the absence of logical connections. Miller himself has said his results do not have "… anything to do with a person's capacity to comprehend printed text," and that his intention was to measure *immediate recall*, not longer term understanding.

David Garvin, a professor at the Harvard Business School and author of *Learning in Action*, asserts that learning is a three-step process. In step one, you **acquire** the information – in this case, by attending a presentation. In step two, you **interpret** the information to determine how it applies to your life or work. And in step three – which is critical but often overlooked, according to Garvin – you **apply** the new information, putting it to use in some way. Interactive exercises can let audience members apply what they have just been given, completing the learning process.

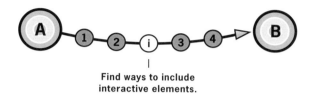

**Find ways to include
interactive elements.**

The simplest form of interaction is question-and-answer, but respondents repeatedly told us through the survey that the traditional last-10-minutes-of-the-presentation Q&A session, while valuable, does not meet their needs. At the very least, presenters should try to check in with the audience periodically through the presentation. Several short Q&A sessions can break up the one-way flow of information, give the audience time to digest what they have just heard, and prevent some attendees from getting lost entirely.

Joel Bradshaw often *starts* his workshops with Q&A, except he's the one asking the questions. "What is one thing you would like to get out of this conversation," he'll ask the audience, "and what is one thing you are concerned about?" This helps Bradshaw adjust his presentation on the fly to meet the needs of the audience.

Several veteran presenters reported showing video clips to break up lectures and get the audience talking. Max Atkinson, who coaches public speakers, will show famous world leaders making speeches and then ask the audience to analyze their technique. "However uncertain people are about their own skills, they are all brilliant as audiences," says Atkinson, and it doesn't take long before his audience is lustily shouting out critiques.

Since Gerry Tabio believes "making lists and making choices" are critical components of creative thinking, he has his audience making lists throughout his workshop. "Within five minutes of sitting down," he says, "people must make lists of facts about themselves and then choose three to use in introducing themselves to the person sitting next to them."

Cliff Atkinson teaches clients how to tell stories with PowerPoint. To open his presentations, he will invite several audience members to participate in a brief (and often funny) improvisational exercise. Using PowerPoint, Cliff will project a single image on a screen (e.g., an airplane) and begin telling a story suggested by that image. After 30 seconds, he'll change the image, and the next person in line must continue the story seamlessly using the new image as inspiration. And on it goes, image after image, audience member after audience member, for about five minutes. "This starts to shift how people see PowerPoint," says Atkinson. "It gets the audience engaged and thinking creatively, and it breaks the ice for those nervous about speaking."

"People can only learn if they do something with it. Questions are interactive, but I don't consider them an interactive exercise. At a minimum, I have them write down something they can do with what they've just heard and then have them share their insight with others as inspiration."

*– KRISTEN GRIMM
SPITFIRE STRATEGIES*

When Terrence McNally, another skilled presenter, talks to organizations about the value of risk-taking, he will ask audience members to think about a time in their life when they took a chance (e.g., asking that certain girl to the prom, asking for a raise, changing careers). Then he will instruct them to find partners and take turns sharing their experiences. This leads to a group discussion that Terrence brings back to the central purpose of the workshop by asking, "Now, what is one risk you plan to take *at work?*"

What all these exercises have in common – and what makes them so effective – is that they are intrinsically related to the subject matter. They are not simply "icebreakers" that may help people relax but have no inherent relationship to the topic at hand. Audience members are cementing what they have learned (or are opening the door to learning) by *doing*, and once the exercise is completed, they are ready to sit down and begin learning some more.

APPEAL TO DIFFERENT LEARNING STYLES

People learn in different ways, and in a room full of public interest professionals, you are bound to have more than one learning style represented. (In fact, several learning styles often operate within a single individual, but some tend to be more dominant than others.) The more learning styles your presentation can appeal to, the better your chances are of reaching everyone in your audience. In his book, *Multiple Intelligences: The Theory in Practice*, Howard Gardner identifies five distinct learning styles, and his categories provide useful guidelines for presenters looking to widen the appeal of their material.

Logical-quantitative: Individuals who learn mostly through this style respond strongly to numbers or deductive reasoning. To find examples of public interest presentations geared to this style, just hold your head up and look around at your next conference or organizational meeting. By that measure, you could easily assume that *everyone* in our sector is primarily a logical-quantitative learner. Just one small problem: They aren't.

Narrational: This kind of learner responds most strongly to stories. When Marc Freedman, president of Civic Ventures, talks about the roles older adults can play in society, he uses a historical narrative to engage his audience. "I'll talk about how the Puritans revered old age, and how they wore white wigs and lied on the census to say they were older than they were," Freedman told us. "I'll talk about how we got from that point to the notion that older people are superfluous or a drain on society, and then give a vision for the future that is more uplifting." As someone who has taught storytelling to public interest professionals across the U.S., I can readily attest to the power of stories when it comes to engaging audiences. When you consider that storytelling has been a constant in human interaction for tens of thousands of years, you have to believe that most people, to at least some extent, are narrational learners. (You can find more on storytelling in the next section.)

Foundational: Some people respond more to broad philosophical arguments as opposed to specific numbers or anecdotes. Robert F. Kennedy, Jr., a senior attorney with the Natural Resources Defense Council, provides plenty of stories and numbers when he talks about the need to protect the environment, but he will often end his speeches with a spiritual message. Kennedy passionately describes the spiritual connection we all share with the earth, and he concludes by saying that destroying the environment is tantamount to ripping out pages from the Bible, Talmud, Koran, or any of our most sacred texts.

Experiential: Interactive exercises are ideal for experiential learners because they naturally crave a hands-on approach. And Joel Bradshaw believes this approach is especially valuable when your audience is comprised of adults. "When you get to be a grown-up, if you are going to go to a training program, the purpose is to change the way you think or act around certain issues," says Bradshaw. "But you don't change behavior intellectually. You have to *learn from the experience.*"

Aesthetic: Imagine for a moment that you had to convince a room full of nonprofit leaders that they would be better served working in a coalition. For most in your audience, telling a story about a similar group that collaborated successfully would probably be the best strategy. But for some, genuine understanding might come from hearing a recording of musicians tuning up – complete with off-key notes and discordant sounds – followed by a recording of an orchestra beautifully performing a symphony. Those individuals who *hear* one difference to understand another are primarily aesthetic learners – people who literally need sensory stimuli to get a "feel" for the subject.

> "A good speaker is a good teacher. Otherwise, what are you doing? You're just pontificating. People should leave smarter and enlightened about the points you came in to talk about."
>
> – LORRAINE MONROE
> LORRAINE MONROE
> LEADERSHIP INSTITUTE

As you think about structuring your presentation to appeal to different learning styles, keep in mind that some audience members will enter a meeting room with a distinct **anti-learning style**. The problem here is not necessarily with you or your subject matter. These individuals are just so deeply entrenched in one way of doing something or of thinking about their work that they are not ready to consider alternatives. (This can also apply to individuals who are generally open-minded, but who happen to be carrying heavy "baggage" from their workplace on the day you see them.)

For full- or part-time "anti-learners," it helps to change the context in which you present your ideas – and the more startling the change, the more likely these people are to lay down their learning shields and start paying attention. When confronted with this kind of audience, Scott Ward, who trains nonprofits in communications strategy and campaigning, will play selected clips from the original "King Kong" movie.

"The first thing I want to do," says Ward, "is separate these people from their biases and have them look at something in a new and fresh way." As an example, Ward points to the activists who come into his workshops believing that their audience is the "general public" – i.e., a large, undifferentiated mass of people who will respond enthusiastically to the same message. Rarely is this the case, Ward says, but he recognizes that simply declaring, "You're wrong!" will not win any converts.

To help these activists think differently, Ward shows clips in which Carl Denham, the character who captures Kong, describes his plans to the various audiences he needs to reach. To the press, Denham spins a romantic tale of "beauty and the beast." To investors, he emphasizes all the money his spectacular exhibition will bring in. Denham is such a shameless hustler that his rants are almost comic, but his tactics are still shrewd – each audience gets a carefully tailored message – and they work … that is, until the title character goes decidedly off-message. "Most people's response to the video is overwhelmingly positive," reports Ward. "What almost everyone says is that it got them to think about messaging in a different way."

Joel Bradshaw takes his audiences through a similar exercise by showing excerpts from "The Music Man," and I begin my storytelling workshop by telling "The Wizard of Oz" story, only I use the jargon-heavy language favored by most public interest professionals. The possibilities for context shifting are endless, and I encourage you to explore them. Those audience members staring at you with crossed arms and furrowed brows will thank you.

TELL STORIES

There's a maxim in public speaking that holds true whether you are addressing five people or 500: *In a two-hour speech, people will remember a two-minute story.* Millennia of conditioning may have something to do with it. As a species, we evolved in storytelling cultures: That's how each clan preserved its most important lessons and ensured they would be passed on to succeeding generations. Even today, we read stories to our children beginning at very early ages, implicitly teaching them to look for the narrative structure that can bring order and meaning to a seemingly random jumble of events (otherwise known as "life").

In previous sections, several expert commentators have already testified to their reliance on stories, and all 20 told us they routinely incorporate stories into their speeches and workshops. Like learning styles, though, storytelling is a subject worthy of entire books – I have written one myself – so we do not intend to offer a comprehensive treatise here. Instead, let me suggest some questions that can help you sharpen the stories you want to tell:

*See **Checklists to Go** for a detachable summary of this section.*

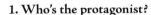

1. Who's the protagonist?
Just as a car needs a driver to get it where it's going, stories need someone to drive the action. This person (or group of people) is called the protagonist, and traditionally structured stories follow protagonists in pursuit of clearly defined goals. To help your audience identify with the protagonist and enter the world of your story, don't be afraid to name names (when appropriate) and provide enough physical description or background to let them see this individual in their mind's eye.

2. What's the hook?
Another technique for drawing people in is beginning the story *where the audience is.* This is your story's "hook" – the description of a place, circumstance, or premise that everyone understands and with which they readily identify. If the subject of your story is global warming, for example, starting with facts about concentrations of carbon dioxide in the atmosphere is not going to engage the average person. On the other hand, asking, "Have you noticed that hurricanes keep getting stronger?" is more likely to get heads nodding.

3. What keeps it interesting?

Predictable stories are boring, and no matter how proud you are of a recent victory, if your story boils down to "We identified a goal, we pursued that goal, we reached that goal!" you're not likely to have audiences rapt with attention. "The stuff of storytelling," says Robert McKee, a renowned Hollywood script doctor, "is the gap between what we think will happen when we take an action, and what actually happens." Take another look at that success story of yours and see if you can recall any barriers or surprises that cropped up along the way. From the listener's perspective, *that's* where the story gets interesting.

4. Where's the conflict?

There is no drama without conflict, and comedies, for that matter, also fall flat without it. Heroic action always comes into sharper focus when juxtaposed against villainous misdeeds, and while your stories will probably not reduce to simple-minded battles of good versus evil, it helps to have clearly defined heroes and villains with different notions of how the story should end.

5. Have you included telling details?

At one of my storytelling workshops, a participant described a small community in West Virginia whose economy collapsed when its primary industry, coal mining, was shut down. The narrator described the place as "a company town," but the image of a controlling and penny-pinching company became vivid when she added that every home was required to turn on its porch lights at 7:00 pm each evening "… because that's how the mining company made sure the streets were lit." A single, telling detail such as that can replace a paragraph or more of description, and good stories have just enough telling details to set the scene and people it with colorful characters.

6. What's the *emotional* hook?

By consenting to read or listen to a story, the audience subconsciously enters into a contract with the storyteller. In return for their time and attention – an increasingly valuable commodity, not so incidentally – they expect more than a recitation of facts. They want an emotional experience that makes the time worthwhile. "Our appetite for a story is a reflection of the profound human need to grasp the patterns of living," says McKee, "not merely as an intellectual exercise, but within a very personal, emotional experience."

7. Is the meaning clear?

Finally, your story should have a crystal clear moral, a reason for taking this particular journey. "We don't need more information," writes Annette Simmons in *The Story Factor*, "We need to know what it means. We need a story that explains what it means and makes us feel like we fit in there somewhere."

The "less is more" rule applies to storytelling as well, something Max Atkinson points out in his book, *Lend Me Your Ears*. "Think of the parable of the Good Samaritan," Atkinson told us. "It's incredibly short. Ronald Reagan's speech on the 40th anniversary of D-Day included stories of less than a minute," he added. One of my favorite stories requires just 500 words:

THE ULTIMATE ELEVATOR STORY

I first heard this story during a workshop on brainstorming. The session leader wanted to illustrate the point that brainstorms can fail to produce the best solution if they begin with the wrong question. Rather than simply state the principle, he told this story, which is true, though names have been changed.

The Ambassador is a 10-story apartment building in San Francisco. A single elevator served the building's tenants, who often speculated that theirs was the slowest elevator in the entire state of California. Eventually, snide comments in the lobby turned into an angry letter to the building's owners, and the time for action was at hand.

The Ambassador was managed by two brothers, Nicholas and Joe. Nicholas, the older and more traditional thinker of the two, immediately saw the straight line connecting problem and solution. He solicited bids from elevator repair companies to modernize the building's machinery and increase the elevator car's speed. The estimates ranged from $150,000 to $200,000, and Nicholas, nodding to tradition once again, picked the one in the middle. For a tidy $175,000 the Ambassador's elevator would receive a brand new motor, controller, hoist machinery, brake, guide rails, counterweight rails, and a spanking new buffer (that thing in the basement which keeps the elevator from crashing through the floor and descending into the center of the earth).

The machinery was installed, and Nicholas used a stopwatch to confirm the elevator was, in fact, a few seconds faster from floor to floor. After allowing two weeks of demonstrably improved service, he surveyed the tenants to ensure satisfaction. Their responses stunned him. Without exception, the tenants saw no difference in service. "Slow as ever," was the commonly heard response. Nicholas was stupefied. His stopwatch didn't lie, and neither did his bank statement, which clearly showed $175,000 less in the building's account.

While Nicholas stewed, Joe – the more creative thinker of the two – contacted a different group of vendors and solicited another round of bids. Within a week, the work Joe had ordered was completed, and now the Ambassador had full-length mirrors on either side of the elevator doors on every floor. Joe circulated a memo to the tenants advising them that technicians had tinkered with the new motor in the elevator (which, in fact, they had not). He assured them that the elevator car was moving faster than ever and solicited their comments. No mention was made of the mirrors.

The tenants' comments were once again unanimous: "A vast improvement," they agreed, with some estimating that waiting times had been cut in half. While Joe beamed, Nicholas fumed. He took out his stopwatch and confirmed that the elevator car was moving no faster than when the new machinery was installed. He pulled Joe aside and demanded an explanation.

"It's simple," Joe explained. "The question wasn't 'How do we make the elevator go faster?' It was 'How do we make time *pass faster* for those who are waiting?'" Joe gestured toward the elevators where a man stood staring into a newly installed mirror, inspecting his suit as he waited. The elevator car arrived, and its doors opened and nearly closed before the man realized his wait was over.

Nicholas finally understood, but he had one more question. "How much for the mirrors?" he asked. "Five thousand, two hundred and sixteen dollars," Joe replied, unable to conceal a smile. "And that was the *high* bid."

Special thanks to Star Elevator in Redwood City, California, and Goldon Windows & Mirrors in Troy, Michigan, for providing the dollar figures used in this story.

Presentations as Stories

Cliff Atkinson believes so strongly in the power of narrative that he designs all his presentations to follow the arc of a story. In his book *Beyond Bullet Points*, Atkinson offers a "Story Template" (pictured here) that follows the basic three-act structure that storytellers have relied on for centuries. By filling in the blanks, you can systematically build an outline for your own story-driven presentations. From there, Atkinson's book explains how to translate your outline into visually interesting slides that let PowerPoint support your storytelling. (For more information and to download a free copy of the template, visit Atkinson's web site, *www.sociablemedia.com*.)

Insert story title and byline here		
Act I: Set up the story		
The setting		
The protagonist		
The imbalance		
The balance		
The solution		
Act II: Develop the action		
5-Minute Column:	15-Minute Column:	45-Minute Column:
Turning point		
Act III: Frame the resolution		
The crisis		
The solution		
The climax		
The resolution		

OPENS AND CLOSES: WORK HARDEST WHERE ATTENTION IS HIGHEST

Whether you are speaking to five or 500, to people who have paid to see you or who have been dragged kicking and screaming from their offices, one principle about audiences remains constant: Their attention will be highest at the beginning and ending of your presentation. (The arrow connecting A to B dips in the middle to represent the inevitable decrease in attention over the course of a typical hour.)

It's just human nature. When we first sit down, we are curious about the speaker and the subject and usually hopeful that the hour (or more) will be time well spent. And when we hear the words, "In conclusion … " even those among us in the deepest reaches of REM sleep will awaken and look to the podium, awaiting those words of wisdom that make it all worthwhile.

Once you have the content of your presentation in place, go back and focus on your opening. This is your opportunity to grab the audience's attention, point it in the direction of your subject, and start building the momentum that will carry everyone in the room all the way to the finish line.

OPENS: DIVE RIGHT IN

"The place that people fall down most is the opening," says Eda Roth, who coaches presenters and public speakers and has observed her share of stumbles. "People throw it away with 'Hello, my name is, here's what I'm going to talk to you about.'" In the parlance of presenting, this is called "ramping up," and it is a practice to be avoided. For the audience, listening to speakers ramp up is almost as exciting as listening to a car engine trying to turn over on a cold morning. In both cases the listener is seated and ready to go (and getting colder by the moment). So get going!

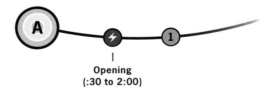

Opening
(:30 to 2:00)

"I get right to it," says Gerry Tabio. "I say, 'Good afternoon everybody. Take out a piece of paper. You're going to make a list.' No introduction. No how are you doing." Joel Bradshaw is equally quick from the starting gate. "Typically, I open with, 'We're going to talk about the 2004 election,' and I show a picture of a woman in front of a TV set sobbing. The audience gets the point right away," and Bradshaw's workshop is off and running.

In *Presenting to Win*, Jerry Weissman says you have to hook your audience within the first 90 seconds at most. Max Atkinson believes you have even less time – 10 to 30 seconds – making it even more imperative that you start strongly. Skilled presenters prepare and rehearse their openings so they can talk without notes and look audience members in the eyes at a time when most of the audience is still looking back.

Some reliable techniques for opening include:

- Telling a story that crystallizes the subject matter of your talk.
- Asking questions that make audience members consider their personal relationship to your subject (e.g., When was the last time you sat through a truly awful presentation?).
- Throwing out a compelling statistic (e.g., there are three times as many places to buy guns in America as there are McDonald's).
- Showing a picture that genuinely lives up to the "thousand words" promise.

See **Checklists to Go**
*for a detachable
summary of this section.*

Keep in mind, however, that diving right in does not exempt you from observing the basic etiquette of presenting. Once you have captured the audience's attention, it is both permissible and advisable to spend a few moments thanking the people who invited you, covering any ground rules for the session (e.g., when it is appropriate to ask questions), and further establishing your credentials if the introduction omitted anything important. But be advised: While this may be proper etiquette, you are still imposing on the good will you have just established with your audience via your opening. So as Terrence McNally likes to say, keep it "brief but brilliant."

And Tell 'em How Long It Will Take

Perhaps the most familiar maxim in presenting is "Tell 'em what you're going to tell 'em, tell 'em, and tell 'em what you told them." To the first part, Jerry Weissman suggests a small addition: Tell 'em *how long* the session will last. "When you establish the endpoint at the beginning of your presentation," he writes in *Presenting to Win*, "instead of plunging your audience headlong into a dark tunnel, they get to see the light at the end while they are still at the entrance. [This demonstrates] you are aware of the value of your audience's time and intend to use it productively."

CLOSES

The close is your chance to cement what audience members have learned and to send them off inspired to act on that new knowledge. Most public interest presenters will end their presentation with their final major point, and if time permits they will entertain questions. This will, indeed, bring the curtain down, but it is not the most effective technique for sending away an audience that is motivated to act.

With audience attention on the rise for the final time, skilled presenters (1) present a summary of the major points, (2) provide time for questions, and then (3) deliver a prepared close, which is distinctly different from the summary.

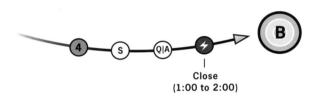

Close
(1:00 to 2:00)

1. The Summary
This is the "tell 'em what you told 'em" part of your presentation: a short reiteration of the major points and a restatement of your overarching message.

2. Question-and-Answer Session
As noted earlier, many of our expert commentators prefer to sprinkle Q&A throughout their presentations to let audience members check in whenever the need arises. Due to time constraints and imposed formats, however, you will often have time for Q&A only toward the end of your session. In these instances, there are several techniques that can help make this time more productive:

- *Do not begin by asking, "Does anybody have any questions?"*
  "It's the worst question anybody can ask," says Gerry Tabio. "It doesn't work." Instead, Tabio recommends, "asking a question that's interesting to answer, such as: I just taught you some techniques. If you were to try this tomorrow, what parts are you not confident in? What fears do you have?" This gets audience members talking, breaks the ice, and starts the flow of questions. Having questions ready to fire at the audience can also help you come evaluation time, says Kristen Grimm. "If you end your Q&A session early because of a lack of questions, you will get a bad evaluation," Grimm warns. "So it's always good to have two or three provocative questions to ask them and get them talking."

- *Prepare for Q&A as you would any other part of the presentation.* Anticipate the questions that are likely to arise and have your answers ready. But don't stop there. "I'm big on the point that it's not enough to know *what* you're going to say," Max Atkinson advises, "you have to know *how* you're going to say it—how to package the message." Write out the answers to anticipated questions in advance. It is not essential to have a complete script on hand, but the writing process will help you find the best language.

- *Coach the audience to ask better questions.* "I preface any Q&A session by letting people know that a lot of questions are appropriate for their own organization, but we are here as a group, so please ask questions that other people can benefit from," says Dynell Garron, who speaks about fundraising. "I say, 'I will generalize your question as needed,' because it's my job before I answer a question to redirect it or reshape it as needed."

- *Do not repeat hostile questions.* "Reposition them," advises Eda Roth. "If someone asks, 'Why are you ripping us off?' you say [to the audience], 'The question has to do with our fee structure, or the amount of work we're doing with this organization.' Listen to the issue, but do not react to the anger. You'll lose credibility."

Above all, *do not end your presentation with Q&A*. "Q&A is potentially the most deadly part of any presentation," says the SPIN Project's Holly Minch. "Some people ask relevant questions and some don't." Even the most experienced presenters can feel the energy draining out of a room during a bad Q&A session. And that's why they prepare a close that will be the last thing the audience hears rather than, "Any more questions?" (Silence.) "Any more questions?" (Someone coughs.) "Thank you." (Polite applause.)

3. The Prepared Closing

As with your opening, lightning must strike here as well. While your audience will accept your glancing at notes during your presentation, they expect you to look them in the eyes when saying farewell. This is your opportunity to tell one more story, restate your message as eloquently as possible (borrowing a quote from a more prominent personage when appropriate), or provide an inspiring vision of the future. Above all, this is your time to tell them in no uncertain terms what you hope they will do with the information they have just received or the skills they have just acquired. "I don't want their final thought to be, 'She's really neat,'" says Nancy Lublin, CEO of Do Something. "I always give a call to action … to get active in *something*."

In my workshop, "Storytelling as Best Practice," I always close with the same words:

"In the long run, numbers numb, jargon jars, and nobody ever marched on Washington because of a pie chart. If you really want to connect with your audience, give them what they're waiting for – what we are always waiting for. Tell them your stories."

A "SOLID" HOUR

A thoughtfully constructed hour is, in reality, anything but solid. Rather, it is a sequence of carefully planned elements that capture the attention of the audience, present key points in a clear and organized fashion, provide opportunities to engage and learn, summarize, cement, and send audience members off – to the next hour, the next session, or back to the real world.

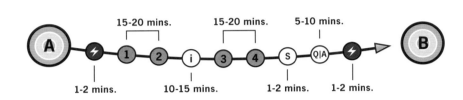

SAMPLE ONE-HOUR SESSION

As mentioned earlier, this is by no means the only way to organize a presentation. But this schematic can serve as a handy reminder of all the pieces you must consider as you assemble your next presentation and plan your audience's journey from A to B.

*See **Checklists to Go** for a detachable summary of this section.*

CHAPTER 3:

IMPROVING YOUR DELIVERY

Just Be Yourself. Only Better.

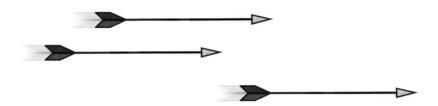

"Good communication is as
stimulating as black coffee,
and just as hard to sleep after."

– Anne Morrow Lindbergh

IMPROVING YOUR DELIVERY
Just Be Yourself. Only Better.

pg. 39

Platform skills – e.g., eye contact, vocal control, how and where you stand on a stage – were the subject of some debate among our expert commentators. On one side was the "Just Be Yourself" camp. Marc Freedman captured the sentiments of this group when he told us, "One of the main lessons I've learned is that the goal is to have your true personality, or a slightly better version, shine through – not to try to be somebody else or use classic public speaking techniques."

On the other hand, several experts asserted that public speaking was a skill that could be learned like any other, which means mastering specific techniques. That goes for novices and veterans alike, says Kristen Grimm. "Bill Clinton did media training as often as he could," she points out. "If it's something that's a major part of your job, you can always be working on it."

As in many such debates, there are elements of truth in both arguments. When public interest professionals get behind the podium, all too often they are "constricted by either their own or a societal sense of professionalism," as Eda Roth puts it. In short, they are *not* themselves, and their presentations suffer for it. Simply relaxing and letting their genuine personalities shine through would undoubtedly be a vast improvement. (Okay, for some people it might be a disaster, but let's stay focused on the larger picture.)

At the same time, a presenter who is comfortable with herself but who doesn't make eye contact with the audience, talks in a whisper, and stands rooted to the podium is not going to win any prizes either. In this case, a little training could quickly polish a diamond in the rough.

I believe that the key word here is *confidence*. When you know your material and also know the best ways to transmit that knowledge from the stage to the audience, it is easier to relax and be yourself. Mastering platform skills can raise your level of confidence, so they are worth studying, practicing, and making your own.

> *"In terms of platform style, I make sure I go in the room feeling really clear and really centered. It reminds me of what Tom Cruise said once. He said that he knows his lines so clearly that all he has to do in the moment is react. I am so prepared and I know the subject, so my job is to stay in the moment and stay present. I'm not worried about what to say next."*
>
> – DYNELL GARRON
> **THE FUNDER'S CHECKLIST**

pg. 40

IMPROVING YOUR DELIVERY
Just Be Yourself. Only Better. – CONT'D

EYE CONTACT: READ THE AUDIENCE, NOT YOUR NOTES

Eye contact can be one of the most powerful tools at a speaker's disposal. Used properly, it can help you connect with your audience, recapture people who are drifting away, and drive home key points. In my travels to conferences across the U.S., I have encountered five different styles of eye contact among public interest presenters. Unfortunately, four of them are bad:

Style #1: "I'm Studying My Shoes"
Somebody must have warned these presenters that eye contact with the audience will cause instantaneous implosion, because they appear bound and determined not to look up. Ever. The only thing their eyes contact during their presentation is their notes.

Style #2: "The Scenic Overlook"
As opposed to practitioners of style #1, these presenters clearly got the message that you have to look up when you speak to an audience. So they look up, up, and over the audience's heads, giving the impression of eye contact without really connecting with anybody.

Style #3: "Sir Glance-a-Lot"
Despite the gender bias in the name, this style boasts male and female practitioners. It is characterized *(look down at notes)* by a constant bobbing of the head *(look up at audience)*, and after a while *(look down at notes)* it can get to be *(look up at audience)* both distracting *(look down at notes)* and annoying *(look up at audience)*. Get the picture?

Style #4: "The Lawn Sprinkler"
You know those rotating sprinkler heads that spray water from one side of a lawn to the other? The kind that makes a "chick-chick-chick" sound as it slowly traces an arc before swinging back to its starting position? Some presenters appear to have drawn inspiration from these devices because their eyes mechanically sweep across the room – looking at but never really connecting with anyone in the audience – before swinging back to the starting point and sweeping across the room again … and again … and again.

Style #5: "One for One"
As you have probably guessed by now, this is the only style of eye contact worth considering. Gerry Tabio referred to it when he told us, "If I'm telling a story that takes two minutes, I tell it to 10 different people one sentence at a time. I never talk to the room. I talk to the people in their eyes."

The key here is to think of your audience not as an undifferentiated mass of people, but individuals who each want to feel like you are speaking directly to them. Eye contact provides that feeling, and you want as many people in your audience as possible to have it. Be advised, though, that a quick glance is not sufficient. You need to stay with each person through an entire sentence or a complete thought, giving each enough time to feel some sense of connection (otherwise known as the "Hey, she's talking to *me!*" moment).

If you find it difficult to look strangers in the eyes, try starting with the friendlier faces – the people who are already smiling and nodding their heads. "Every audience has them," says Terrence McNally. "Just as there are great presenters, there are great audience members, and if you find them, it's going to make your job easier." It can also be helpful to make small talk with audience members in advance so that some of them will not be complete strangers when you take to the stage.

"Presentations fail when people are not reading the audience," says Dynell Garron. "Bad presenters are not really looking up, not trying to see if the audience cares." So look up, look at one person at a time, and show them you are interested in their reactions. They will show you greater interest in return.

What Happens When Nobody's Looking
"I did a study a few years ago for an American company that thought it could save millions of dollars a year with video conference links," says Max Atkinson. "What happened was that people in the same room as the speaker behaved like an ordinary audience, but people who thought they couldn't be seen by the speaker – *their behavior was abysmal.*" And how does Atkinson account for the difference? "They were released from the constraints of eye contact, so they were making coffee and reading newspapers! The norm for good audience behavior is: Thou shalt look attentive. If the speaker never looks or is not [physically] in the same room, the audience relaxes and does crossword puzzles."

pg. 42

IMPROVING YOUR DELIVERY
Just Be Yourself. Only Better. – CONT'D

VOCAL CONTROL: KNOW YOUR KNOBS

Like your eyes, your voice is an instrument that can help convey meaning and engage your audience. Most public interest presenters that I have heard, however, apparently believe this instrument has only two settings: "Speaker-Blowing Loud," to be used when they want the audience's attention, and "White Noise Monotone" for the body of their remarks.

Skilled speakers know that their voice is a much more sophisticated instrument with three different "control knobs" that can be adjusted in countless combinations:

Volume
Gradually increasing the loudness of your voice sends a message to your audience, imbuing your text with greater importance, urgency, and emotion. Deliberately dropping your volume below normal speaking levels can also call more attention to parts of your presentation, because a lowered voice can suggest confidentiality. (After all, when someone starts talking softly, don't you instinctively expect to hear something juicy?)

Amateur speakers raise their voices and pound the podium to get attention. More skilled orators recognize that this can wear out an audience, and that varying their attention-getting vocal techniques will serve them better over time.

Speed
Slowing down and placing more emphasis on each word can also call greater attention to certain parts of your presentation. (Stop entirely and you can count on people looking up.) This can be a more powerful technique than increasing volume because it implies you don't have to shout – the words carry the weight for themselves, but you are serving them up a bit more deliberately just to make sure everyone gets the point.

Deliberately increasing the pace of your presentation can let audiences know "this part is worth hearing but we're not going to dwell on it," but be careful: Speaking too fast for too long without pausing long enough to let the audience digest can lead to information overload. High speed can also be associated with nervousness, so always use the accelerator with care.

> "If something is really important, I pause and get softer because it emphasizes the importance of what I'm saying. People have to listen harder."
>
> – JOEL BRADSHAW
> **JOEL BRADSHAW ASSOCIATES**

Tone

Serious, sarcastic, playful, bored – your voice can also convey a range of emotions. Changing your tone can completely change the meaning of your words. For example, consider the sentence: "Now there's a good idea." Said one way, it can mean, "Finally, someone has come up with a useful suggestion." Said another, it means, "That's the stupidest thing I've ever heard." And spoken in a neutral tone, it can leave the listener wondering what the speaker is really thinking. Since you probably want your audience to know precisely what you are thinking, take a moment to ask yourself if your tone is consistently conveying the meaning you intend.

Presenters who do not alter their volume, speed, or tone, produce a monotonous white noise that can gradually lull audiences to sleep, or at least send them reaching for their BlackBerrys. It is the variation in these qualities that makes for interesting listening, and purposeful variations are one mark of gifted orators.

BODY LANGUAGE – WHAT IS YOURS SAYING?

Escaping the Podium Prison

When Bill Clinton debated George H.W. Bush, there was a memorable moment in which Clinton left his podium to stand closer to an audience member who had just asked a question. The move was classic Clinton – brushing aside the vestiges of formality to be "closer to the people" – and an excellent example of one effective way to handle yourself on stage.

A podium is fine for holding a microphone, your notes and a glass of water, but it can also become a barrier between speakers and their audience. Your entire body is potentially an instrument of expression, but a podium can conceal most of that instrument. So why hide behind it or allow it to keep you rooted in place? Wearing a wireless microphone can free you to talk more directly to audience members, point at items on the screen for greater emphasis, and generally communicate more like a human being than a lecturer.

Of course, there will be instances when the room set-up or audio/visual equipment absolutely requires your sustained presence at the podium. Even on these occasions, though, your body can work with your eyes and voice to energize your material and engage the audience. "I try to project movement and energy from behind the podium with large gestures and very small, subtle gestures," says Geoffrey Canada, president and CEO of Harlem Children's Zone. "The audience begins to look at you differently when you use both. You can raise your hands or just raise an eyebrow and they'll zoom right in on your face."

"If your goal is persuasion, you have to convey a sense of conviction and passion yourself. No one is going to be swayed by someone who does not, himself, seem strongly committed to the proposition. That does not mean table thumping, but a good strong look in the eye, use of pauses, even talking quietly can do it – as long as it's heartfelt."

– LILYAN WILDER
AUTHOR
7 Steps to Fearless Speaking

"I use a lavaliere so I can move. People don't love a stick who reads."

– LORRAINE MONROE
LORRAINE MONROE
LEADERSHIP INSTITUTE

pg. 44

IMPROVING YOUR DELIVERY
Just Be Yourself. Only Better. – CONT'D

Loosen Up and Open Up

Thanks to her background in theatre, Eda Roth is intimately familiar with the relationship between how people carry themselves on stage and the non-verbal messages they project to the audience. When she coaches public interest clients, she told us, her main challenge is getting them to loosen up and open up. "The same people who are very expressive at their children's soccer games are not as expressive in their professional lives," she says.

To help clients relax and open up, Roth conducts an exercise in which presenters must start their talk by literally running into the room and exclaiming, "I have the most incredible thing to tell you!" Most clients will respond by jogging to the podium with an embarrassed look on their faces, but Roth sends them back and demands a full-out sprint. "I want to break through the constrictions of so-called professionalism and get them to open up to the possibility of a bigger and more visceral expression," she explains.

> "An audience wants one thing above all, which is for the **person** to show up."
>
> – PAUL HAWKEN
> NATURAL CAPITAL
> INSTITUTE

Much to her clients' relief, Roth doesn't expect them to incorporate the running start into their actual presentations. "It's a matter of stretching out *a lot* so that when the personality snaps back, it's a little larger than it was," she says. In a similar exercise, Roth will ask presenters to identify the emotion – excitement, anger, empathy, frustration – that is central to their talk. Once they have it, she instructs them to make their points *saying exactly what they feel,* shorn of any euphemisms or diplomatic language. This no-holds-barred exercise helps presenters feel the emotion more clearly, and that's what Roth wants them to remember when they eventually put the diplomatic language back into their talk. That "body memory" will make them more expressive, supporting their words with the right non-verbal messages as well.

Wordsmiths Take Heart (Maybe It Really *Is* What You Say)

In the 1960s, UCLA professor Albert Mehrabian conducted research to measure the significance of non-verbal cues in communications. From a series of tests involving face-to-face conversations, he concluded that 38% of communication is inflection and tone of voice, 55% is facial expression, and only 7% *is based on what you actually say.*

Since then, many communications consultants and public speaking coaches have cited this study when telling clients, "It's not *what* you say but *how* you say it." Unfortunately, like George Miller's "Magic Number 7," Mehrabian's measly 7% does not necessarily hold for all forms of communication.

In Mehrabian's study, subjects who played the role of "listener" had only one task: to determine how the "speaker" *felt* about them. In addition, the speakers and listeners were complete strangers, so there was no additional context for the listeners to draw on. Given that most audience members will have some knowledge of the subjects and speakers they come to hear, and that their intent is more to learn than to figure out if the speaker likes them, it seems that where presentations are concerned, Mehrabian's findings, while fascinating, probably do *not* apply.

HUMOR: THE FUNNY THING ABOUT BEING FUNNY

People love to laugh, so humor can be a powerful tool for presenters. It can start presentations off on the right foot, provide needed pick-me-ups as you roll along, and send your audience off with a smile. It's also a great way to keep their attention, because once a presenter has established that she's got a good sense of humor (and isn't afraid to use it), everyone will listen more closely for the next good line.

If being funny is part of who you are, then it is perfectly natural for humor to be part of your presentation. Having written for network television sitcoms ("Dinosaurs" on ABC and "The Nanny" on CBS), I am very comfortable with comedy and look for appropriate ways to incorporate it into my speeches and workshops. My speech, "Storytelling as Best Practice," offers a useful example of how I try to use humor not only to entertain, but to illustrate a substantive point as well.

At the beginning of the speech, I note that nonprofits have excellent stories to tell, but they tend to tell them badly, often weighing them down with excessively technical language, acronyms, and statistics galore. To demonstrate, I invite the audience to play a game: I announce that I am going to tell a story that everyone in the room knows, only I am going to tell it like someone from a nonprofit would. The challenge for the audience: Decode the jargon and identify the story.

With appropriately bland PowerPoint slides to back me up, I then provide a highly condensed plot summary of the heartwarming American classic, "The Wizard of Oz," except in my version the heart has been surgically removed and the story has been re-titled, "The Role of Family and Community in Mentoring Alienated Youth in the American Midwest."

One day, an at-risk youth from a blended family in the economically depressed farm belt is rendered unconscious during an extreme weather event.

When she awakens, she undertakes a long, hazardous journey to a distant, mineral-based metropolitan center. Along the way, she is accompanied by three variously challenged and apparently homeless adults while also being pursued by a malevolent person of color – in this case, green.

Just before she reaches her destination, she briefly struggles with opium addiction, but fortunately that problem is cured by snow.

By this point, everyone in the audience has recognized the story, so the narration abruptly ends there, often drowned out by laughter. More importantly, though, a serious point has been made in a way that lets audience members recognize their foibles and laugh at themselves – which is probably preferable to the opening I used in previous versions of the speech: "Hey folks: Your storytelling sucks."

"Laughter is not only evidence of audience enjoyment or approval, but is also a powerful spur to continued attentiveness."

– MAX ATKINSON
AUTHOR
Lend Me Your Ears

Improving Your Delivery
Just Be Yourself. Only Better. – cont'd

Two words of warning before you start using your license to kill (comedically speaking, that is): Your subject matter or the circumstances of your presentation may set limits on what is appropriate. (Just ask anyone who spoke publicly in the days and weeks immediately following 9/11.) So always proceed with caution. And if you do not feel that humor is your strong suit, please do not feel compelled to start with a joke just because some book claims that comedy is sure-fire stuff for speaking success. Few things are more cringe inducing than watching a humor-challenged presenter trying to tell a joke. It's just *painful*. So spare the audience, spare yourself, and get on with it.

CHAPTER 4:

PowerPoint Is Your Friend

Seriously.

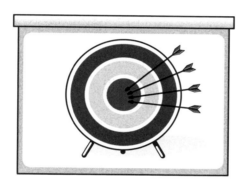

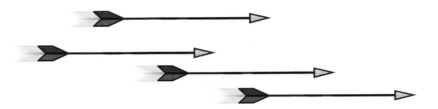

"Using PowerPoint is like having a loaded
AK-47 on the table: You can do very bad
things with it."

– PETER NORVIG
  CREATOR OF THE POWERPOINT
  GETTYSBURG ADDRESS

No question about it: PowerPoint was a bargain. First developed under the name "Presenter" by a company called Forethought, the program and its parent were both acquired by Microsoft in 1987 for $14 million – chump change for Bill Gates, and a steal considering subsequent sales that have landed PowerPoint on an estimated 400 million computers worldwide.

What remains a hotly debated question, though, is whether or not using PowerPoint is a bargain with the devil. When presenters turn their material over to the AutoContent Wizard – cookie-cutter software that spits out endless slides with bullets, clip art, and colorful backgrounds – are they condemning their presentation and whoever sees it to a slow and painful death? Or is this actually a case of mistaken identity where a poorly used (but essentially blameless) tool has been subjected to criticism that belongs elsewhere?

Numerous experts from academia, the business community, and other sectors have weighed in heavily on these questions. Edward Tufte, professor emeritus at Yale University, is one of PowerPoint's harshest critics. In an essay entitled "PowerPoint is Evil" (*Wired*, September 2003), Tufte wrote:

> *"In a business setting, a PowerPoint slide typically shows 40 words, which is about eight seconds' worth of silent reading material. With so little information per slide, many, many slides are needed. Audiences consequently endure a relentless sequentiality, one damn slide after another. When information is stacked in time, it is difficult to understand context and evaluate relationships. Visual reasoning usually works more effectively when relevant information is shown side by side."*

Seth Godin, author, entrepreneur, and self-described "agent of change," prefers to dwell on the upside potential of this ubiquitous software. "PowerPoint presents an amazing opportunity," Godin writes in his e-book, *Really Bad PowerPoint (And How to Avoid It)*. "You can use the screen to talk emotionally to the audience's right brain (through their eyes), and your words can go through the audience's ears to talk to their left brain. That's what Steven Spielberg does. It seems to work for him."

Who's right? Having sat through enough mind-numbing PowerPoint presentations to last several lifetimes, I understand why its critics are so venomous. But when it comes to pointing fingers, I think Jerry Weissman has the proper perspective. "Trying to blame PowerPoint and make it controversial, as Edward Tufte tries to do, is like blaming the pen company, Mont Blanc, for bad handwriting," Weissman told us. "It's not the pen. It's the *penmanship*."

Boredom by the Pound

"Last year, I did a calculation of how much PowerPoint is costing the British economy each year. If you take the number of managers in the country earning 30,000 pounds a year or more, attending one presentation for one hour a week, and you know 90% of the presentations bore them and they get nothing out of them ... the answer is 7.8 billion pounds [or roughly 14.2 billion US dollars]. And that's not including the time people spend preparing the slides, the travel costs to the venue, or the hire of rooms. The real cost is very much higher."

– Max Atkinson
Author
Lend Me Your Ears

POWERPOINT IS YOUR FRIEND
Seriously. – CONT'D

"I need someone well versed in the art of torture—do you know PowerPoint?"

In short, the fault, dear reader, is not in our slides, but in ourselves. PowerPoint is a tool like any other, and if you know how to use it properly, you can produce visuals that add value to your presentation. Real know-how, though, goes beyond simply learning how to insert some groovy animation or send text flying around a page. (Those skills more properly belong in the "a little knowledge is a dangerous thing" category.)

Having spent countless hours working and experimenting with this software, I have learned several techniques that take advantage of PowerPoint's greatest assets – and some are as easy as pressing a single key. Before designing your next slide show, I encourage you to consider the recommendations below and to try some of these techniques for yourself.

FIRST, ACCEPT WHAT POWERPOINT IS <u>NOT</u>.

A PowerPoint presentation is *not* a document. Brochures, reports, memos or other printed materials can do the heavy lifting of information transfer between you and your audience. Your presentation – whether 10 minutes or two hours long – should neither resemble nor recapitulate printed matter. It is also *not* an outline projected on screen to help you remember the key points of your talk. If you need prompts, carry index cards.

Your time at the podium is an opportunity to convey the essence of your proposal, shine a spotlight on key points of a report, or tell stories that bring your issue to life. And the central purpose of your PowerPoint is to provide visual elements that more clearly explain, more dramatically depict, and more emotionally emphasize each point you wish to make. Bearing that in mind …

See **Checklists to Go**
*for a detachable
summary of this section.*

SAY THE WORDS. SHOW THE PICTURES.

As Seth Godin astutely observed above, the people in your audience have two channels for processing information: visual and auditory. These channels work simultaneously, so audience members are perfectly capable of looking at a slide, listening to the presenter, and making sense from both streams of information. These same people can run into trouble, however, when they have too much information to process at one time.

How much is too much? In 1998, Richard Mayer conducted a series of tests on college students to answer this question. Mayer created two sets of slides to teach students how lightning storms develop. The first set was comprised only of images (*see figure 1*) and as each slide was shown to the students, a narrator explained what the image was depicting. The second set of slides had the same images, but in this set the explanation was printed on the slide for the student to read (*see figure 2*). No narration accompanied these slides.

"As air in the updraft cools, water vapor condenses into water droplets and forms a cloud."

FIGURE 1

FIGURE 2

After reviewing the slides, the students were tested for retention of the information they had just been given. Even though the images and explanations were identical, the students who saw the images and *heard* the narrated explanation retained more than the students who saw the images and *read* the explanation themselves. Mayer repeated the test four times and obtained the same result every time. His conclusion: Presenting a picture with narration allows the two information processing channels to work collaboratively. Presenting a picture with text overloads the visual channel (while ignoring the auditory channel) and can actually hinder learning.

Narration + Image

"As air in the updraft cools, water vapor condenses into water droplets and forms a cloud."

FIGURE 1

Narration + Text in Image

As air in the updraft cools, water vapor condenses into water droplets and forms a cloud.

"As air in the updraft cools, water vapor condenses into water droplets and forms a cloud."

FIGURE 3

To further test this theory, Mayer ran another side-by-side experiment with one critical difference. As before, the first set of slides showed images only accompanied by voice narration. The second set showed images with text, but this time narration was included as well (*see figure 3*). Once again, the students who saw the first set of slides retained more than those viewing the second set.

From these results, Mayer concluded that students viewing the second set of slides were hindered by *two* problems. As before, their visual processing channel was overloaded with information. And instead of opening a second channel for learning, the narrator's voice further aggravated the situation. When people read text on a screen while a presenter intones those same words aloud, Mayer asserts, the audience's tendency is to listen for differences to determine if the printed and spoken words are, in fact, the same. And that means the audience is *not* focusing on the content!

"When making a multimedia presentation consisting of animation and words," Mayer writes in his book, *Multimedia Learning*, "present the words as narration rather than on-screen text." Like any rule, there are exceptions here as well, but as a general guideline for the design of PowerPoint slides, Mayer's advice is worth heeding.

DESIGN OUTSIDE THE (WHITE) BOX.

Most presentations I see use PowerPoint's default white background for each slide. This projects the familiar white box on the screen, causing so many presentations to look essentially the same. Even when presenters discover color backgrounds (or, heaven forefend, built-in templates), their images and text remain trapped inside a box.

When you design slides with a black background, however, the LCD projector puts nothing on the screen except the images and text you choose. This allows you to create slides with no apparent borders while focusing the viewer's attention precisely where you want it.

Consider the slide "Goals" (*figure 4*) at right, which appeared in a presentation for the Nurse-Family Partnership (a nationwide program that sends registered nurses into the homes of low-income, first-time mothers). In many ways, this is your typical, garden variety public interest slide: bland title, three bullet points, an image that screams "Stock photography!", the organization's logo in the corner – and all of it packaged in the numbingly familiar white box. No, it won't send anyone screaming from the room, but it is not exactly eye-catching either.

FIGURE 4

Now consider this redesigned version, "Three Goals" (*figure 5*). The title, while still on the bland side, conveys more information. The Hallmark card photo has been replaced by a larger black-and-white image that has a more authentic, documentary quality. Since the logo consumes space without adding any new information, it has been deleted. (If the audience does not know what organization is presenting to them, you are already in a deeper hole than any logo can fill). Most dramatic of all, by switching to a black background, the text and image become the only items on the screen, and eyes will naturally gravitate to them.

FIGURE 5

USE STYLE TO CONVEY SUBSTANCE.

Nonprofits, foundations, government agencies – they come in all shapes and sizes with enormous differences in their public personae. So why do their PowerPoint presentations look so similar? The problem is not with the software. There is enough flexibility built into PowerPoint to create a look to match your organization – beyond simply slapping a logo onto each slide – and to bring greater clarity to each presentation.

Conveying Identity

Roca is a nonprofit organization based in Chelsea, Massachusetts, that works primarily with adolescents who need help finding their place in the community. To do this, Roca's staff works diligently to instill four core values in the youth they serve: belonging, generosity, competence and independence. Roca runs a community center as the hub of its operation, but its staff often takes to the streets, going to the kids when the kids will not come to them. As Molly Baldwin, Roca's executive director, will readily tell you, the work is rewarding, but it comes with a lot of rough edges.

FIGURE 6

When Roca's staff used PowerPoint to describe their programs, they would show the slide "Roca's values …" (*figure 6*) when they reached the four values. The slide is a classic example of excellent programmatic work undermined by pedestrian presentation. The text is clear and concise, and it leaves plenty of room for more powerful visual elements, but the images chosen use less than half the available space. For the audience, details in the images will be difficult to see, and the relationship of each picture to the core values is unclear. Putting everything inside a blue box does little to distinguish the overall look of the presentation from other nonprofit slide decks.

Given the opportunity to revamp this presentation, I began by looking for design elements that would convey the grittiness and "rough edges" of Roca's daily operation. I searched its image library to find pictures with strong emotional appeal. I only used black-and-white versions (even when color was available) because these help viewers "see the story" in the image instead of being distracted by an array of colors. I used PowerPoint's "scribble" line to create irregular frames for the key words in each slide. And by selecting a black background, I created slides that broke out of the familiar four-wall frame while focusing viewer attention on the important elements.

Because the four values are so central to Roca's work, I decided to create separate slides for each value (*figures 7–10*). This allowed me to choose photographs that would portray and visually reinforce each value, and with just one word on each slide, I was able to run large versions of each image. Expanding one slide into four also made the presenter's visual backdrop more dynamic and interesting without lengthening the presentation.

FIGURE 7

FIGURE 8

FIGURE 9

FIGURE 10

Conveying Structure

The Partnership for Climate Action (PCA) is a collaboration of international companies and an environmental organization working to reduce greenhouse gas emissions worldwide. When PCA's representatives recruit new businesses, they use a PowerPoint presentation that covers a lot of territory – six substantial agenda items, as you can see in this slide (*figure 11*). The material is complex and it is easy for viewers to get lost in all the science and statistics of global warming. In designing this presentation, consequently, my overarching goal was clarity.

FIGURE 11

To help audience members keep track of their place in the presentation, I created what resembles a horizontally oriented "navigation bar" on the left side of each slide. I condensed the agenda items to single words and stacked these inside the bar. As the PCA spokesperson covers each item, its corresponding key word appears in bright white (e.g., "SCIENCE" in *figure 12*) while the remaining items remain darkened.

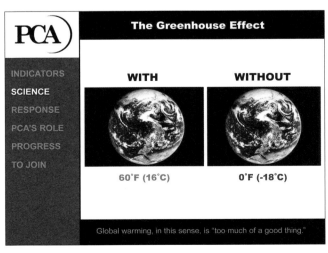

FIGURE 12

I used a similar approach to keep structure explicit in a presentation for the Edna McConnell Clark Foundation (EMCF). EMCF focuses its grantmaking on youth development, and the foundation has chosen to concentrate its philanthropy on a relatively small number of high-performing nonprofits. Its philosophy is straightforward: Find what works, and help it grow so it can serve more people.

When president Nancy Roob describes EMCF's approach to other philanthropies, her talk has three distinct sections: First, she recounts lessons learned from the foundation's experience with current and recent grantees; second, she shares results from a research study EMCF commissioned about the opportunities and challenges of helping nonprofits "scale up"; and finally, she enumerates the points which she hopes audience members will take away from the presentation.

As with PCA, I created a template for each slide that would help audience members visually track their place in Roob's presentation (*figure 13*). I used a black background and stripped the titles of the three sections of Roob's talk across the top of each slide. By placing a white box with rounded corners around a section head, I created a "tab" that would pop up as Roob began each new segment. (Admittedly, this design runs dangerously close to the dreaded white box, but I believe that the visualized structure, use of strong images, and limited text work together to lift this look out of the ordinary.)

FIGURE 13

USE ANIMATION TO CONTROL THE FLOW OF INFORMATION AND CONVEY MEANING.

The version of PowerPoint that I use (PowerPoint 2004 for Mac) offers more than 50 ways to animate text. To the novice, this can seem like an embarrassment of riches, but presentations that incorporate a rich variety of animation techniques are usually just embarrassing. Words or images that fly onto the screen, stretch like rubber, drop into place like a bouncing ball, or take some other fancy route to their ultimate destination are almost always nothing more than eye candy that adds empty calories to the viewer's "meal."

Which is not to say that all animations are pointless. Used thoughtfully, animated words and images can help you dole out information to audience members in digestible pieces, keep their attention focused where it belongs, and even add another layer of meaning to each slide.

Animating bullets to control information flow

When a slide with multiple bullet points (such as the agenda slide for PCA on page 56) appears on-screen, audience members will automatically read all the bullets, even while the presenter is still talking about bullet #1. Human nature is at work once again, but it creates problems in the transmission of information from presenter to audience. As the audience members read ahead, they invariably tune out the spoken explanation of bullet #1, so they may miss critical information right from the start. And once they know where the presenter is headed in subsequent bullets, they may tune out the remaining comments until the next slide appears – more valuable information lost.

Animation can help presenters avoid this problem. By bringing in each bullet point with a simple effect (e.g., appear, fade in, peek in from left), the presenter places on the screen only the information he or she wants the audience to see. Subsequent points remain invisible until the spoken explanation is finished. Audience members can still find other things to read if they have to, but at least you won't be providing the distraction yourself.

Animating graphic elements to deliver complex information gradually

There may be occasions when you need to show a map, chart, or other graphic that concentrates a large amount of information on a single slide. Simply showing the complete picture all at once can overwhelm the audience, and even if you take the time to explain how all the pieces fit together, you run the same risk as the presenter who displays all his bullets at once. While you are here, the audience is there, and your verbal explanation may be tuned out as viewers try to make sense of the visual information on their own.

In my workshop "Storytelling as Best Practice," I display this slide (*figure 14*) to illustrate the basic structure that has been used in stories from the earliest myths and fables to last

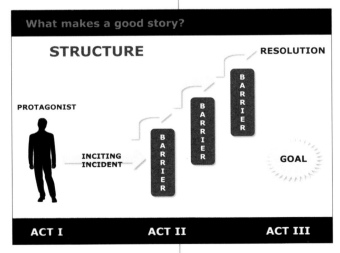

FIGURE 14

week's episode of "Desperate Housewives." As you can see, there is a fair amount of visual information in this one slide, and every part of the schematic requires explanation. Were I to show this slide (precisely as you see it on page 58) at the beginning of the structure discussion, I can guarantee that my audience's eyes would be darting from image to image, inspecting different parts of the slide no matter where I happened to be focused.

To keep them where I want them, I use animation to gradually build this schematic right before their eyes. As I explain that a story begins when a protagonist is launched in pursuit of a goal, the graphic elements you see on figure 15 appear. With only these elements present, I can spend a little more time defining exactly what a protagonist is, what constitutes a goal, and why we need some recognizable event (i.e., the "inciting incident") to set the story in motion.

Once this groundwork is laid, I explain that stories become interesting when problems (or "barriers") appear, forcing protagonists to find new paths to their goals. The more barriers, the more interesting the story becomes, I tell them, and on that cue the blue barriers and light blue arrows appear to illustrate the "rising action" of the story (*figure 16*).

Finally, I explain that a story ends when the protagonist finds his (or her) way around the final barrier and arrives at the resolution – which may or may not be the intended goal but nevertheless concludes the story and makes its meaning clear. At this point, the final graphic pieces of the puzzle fall into place (*figure 17*), including a black bar at the bottom of the slide that shows how this schematic translates into the classic three-act structure of play and screenwriting.

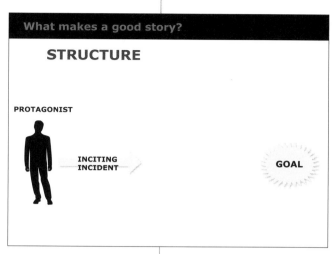

FIGURE 15

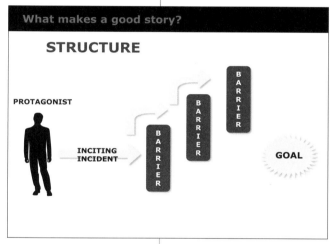

FIGURE 16

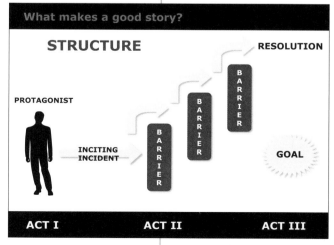

FIGURE 17

FIGURE 18

FIGURE 19

FIGURE 20

Animating text to convey meaning

When text moves around on a slide, there should be a valid reason. (And just in case you were wondering: "It looks cool" is *not* a valid reason.) In many of my PowerPoint presentations, I will use verbatim quotes from books, magazines, web sites or other sources. When I do, I will often incorporate an animation to visually emphasize the use of source material.

During a workshop on PowerPoint, for example, I cite a quote from Jerry Weissman's excellent book, *Presenting to Win*. Since I often find it valuable to let audience members read quotes for themselves (thereby hearing the words in their favorite voice – their own), I will show the entire quote on the screen. This occurs with the help of an animation, depicted in the slide sequence at left.

When the slide first appears, audience members see only the book cover (*figure 18*). After a two-second pause (giving them sufficient time to digest the title), the quote animates with the command PEEK IN FROM LEFT. In this way, the quote literally emerges from the book (*figure 19*) before finding its place to the right of the cover (*figure 20*). Once the quote is on-screen, not so incidentally, I remain silent so the audience can read it without me overloading their learning channels.

If this looks like a blinding flash of the obvious ("The quote comes out of the book. Big deal."), be advised that it's not always so obvious to the audience, especially during a presentation in which they will hear several quotes from a number of different sources. Before using this technique, I would often hear audience members attribute quotes to me even though I had named the original sources. Showing the source and using animation to demonstrate that *the quote comes from this source* has eliminated this problem.

UNIFY ELEMENTS TO CREATE A VISUAL HIERARCHY.

Like a well-designed print advertisement or billboard, a PowerPoint slide should capture attention like a stop sign and direct it like a road map. Too often, however, the slides in nonprofit presentations are all over the road. They may appear at a glance to have the minimum daily adult requirements – a title, bullet points, picture and caption – but the overall design does not tell the viewer where to look first, second, third, etc. There is too much visual clutter. And as a result, the eye wanders, then the mind wanders, then the viewer wanders right out of the room.

"Clutter and confusion are failures of design, not necessarily the amount of information," says Edward Tufte in his seminar, "Presenting Data and Information." In many cases, by simply rearranging and visually prioritizing the same elements, a poorly designed slide can be transformed into an eye-catching thing of beauty.

Environmental Defense, a national environmental organization, used this slide (*figure 21*) to depict the ecological damage caused by clearcutting forests in the Western Sierra Mountains. The overall design of the slide is seemingly clean and professional, but its visual power is undermined by two problems: There are too many items competing for the eye's attention, and the most important item is not prioritized.

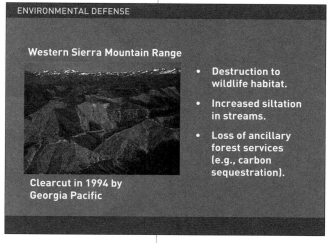

FIGURE 21

Like many organizations (nonprofit and otherwise), Environmental Defense uses a standard template for all its PowerPoint presentations. This template was one product of a comprehensive branding effort, which is laudable for its intent to unify the visual representations of the group's work. For PowerPoint, however, the template (like almost all such templates I have seen) puts information on every slide that adds very little to the presentation while denying space to elements that legitimately require it.

Branding is important, but an organization can remain true to its brand by using the designated color palette, font, and basic design style *without* slavishly imposing unnecessary graphics on every single PowerPoint slide. This was the basic philosophy behind my redesign efforts (*figure 22*). First, by eliminating the organization's name, logo, and the blue bars on the top and bottom of the slide, I created space so the most important element – the picture of the clearcut mountainside – could become the dominant visual. After that, I used Environmental Defense's prescribed color and font to present the text in a box that is clearly secondary to the picture. Finally, I animated the name of the mountain range, the date of its clearcutting, and the three bullets so they would appear *only* as the speaker reached each point.

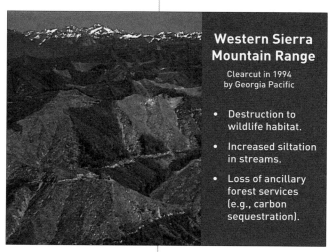

FIGURE 22

DISCOVER THE LITTLE MIRACLES.

As I said earlier, PowerPoint can perform some very useful tasks at the touch of just one or two keys.

To bring the audience's attention back to the podium:
Given the choice of looking at the speaker or a slide, audiences generally choose the slide. Don't take it personally: If they can hear you, they will not feel obligated to look at you, too. Sometimes, though, you need their undivided attention. PowerPoint gives you the tool: the letter B key. Press it once while in VIEW SHOW mode, the screen will go black, and every eye in the room will return to you. Press it again and your slide magically reappears – and every head will turn back to the screen. (You can achieve a similar effect by pressing the letter W key – which will turn the screen white – but I have found that audiences may be distracted by the white box, possibly because they expect something will eventually appear inside it.)

To display any slide at any time:
Most public interest presenters I meet labor under the misconception that PowerPoint only allows users to move forward or backward through a presentation one slide at a time. If an audience member asks to see a slide shown earlier, these presenters dutifully page backwards one slide after another, often having to click through several animations within a single slide. Not only is this boring for the rest of the audience, it is an unnecessary waste of time.

To jump to any slide at any time, simply type the number of the slide you wish to display (using the number row on the keyboard) and hit the ENTER key. To return to the last slide displayed before the jump, type its number and hit ENTER. Of course, this requires having a numbered list of all your slides handy, but for that small amount of extra preparation, you can move with complete freedom from one end of your slide deck to the other.

To access "bonus slides":
As you plan a presentation, you may find yourself with slides you are ambivalent about using. On the one hand, you might have a group of slides that will really drive a point home. On the other, if the audience does not find that point fascinating to begin with, you will probably want to get through that part of your talk as quickly as possible. So you are left in a quandary: Build in one slide or more?

The technique of jumping to any slide at any time provides your solution. When you have slides that seem optional, place them at the end of your presentation. Include these "bonus slides" on your numbered list, and – using the instructions above – you can access them as needed and then jump right back to where you were.

This kind of planning can also serve you well during Q&A. If you have given a presentation several times, you probably know what questions will arise throughout your talk or especially during Q&A. So create slides specifically to address those questions (when you need visual support, that is) and add them to the back of your deck. If the predicted questions arise, you will appear exceptionally prepared. And if they do not, nobody in the audience will be the wiser.

CHAPTER 5:

THE SMALL STUFF

(It's Worth Sweating)

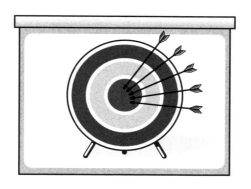

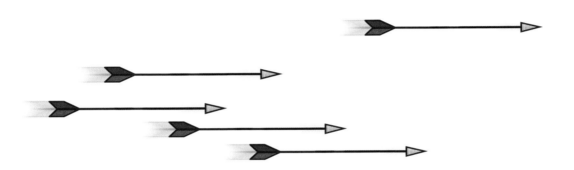

"To be really great in little things,
to be truly noble and heroic in the
insipid details of everyday life, is a
virtue so rare as to be worthy
of canonization."

– Harriet Beecher Stowe

Even when you have a presentation that is beautifully tailored to the audience and you are prepared to deliver it with enthusiasm and skill, you can still be undone by the little things. Experienced presenters know that their preparations for a talk are not complete until they have done their homework on the following items:

LOGISTICS

Despite having their expectations lowered by a steady barrage of bad presentations, audiences still have some minimum requirements that must be met. They expect to hear your voice and see your visuals without unduly straining their ears and eyes. If they have to take notes, they expect a level surface to write on. And they prefer room temperatures that avoid the arctic and equatorial extremes.

*See **Checklists to Go** for a detachable summary of this section.*

Since audiovisual equipment, room setups, and the event-planning expertise of your hosts will vary widely from location to location, it is incumbent upon you to nail down in advance all the details that help ensure a smooth, professional presentation:

Room Setup
If you want all audience members facing forward with tables in front of them, request "classroom style" seating. If you plan on breaking the audience into smaller discussion groups, round tables (or "rounds" in event-planning parlance) are preferable, and these also provide a level surface for note taking. And if note taking is not essential and you prefer to have the audience consolidated in a more intimate space, then "theatre style" seating (i.e., parallel rows of chairs only) is the setup to request.

Light and Sound
Rooms with bright lights that cannot be dimmed or windows without shades can ruin presentations that rely on projected visuals. If you use PowerPoint, ask the meeting organizer if either (a) the LCD projector is sufficiently powerful to overcome any level of room lighting, or (b) lights can be lowered to accommodate PowerPoint or similar visuals. By asking in advance, you give the organizer time to shift the location of your presentation, if necessary, or to ensure that the right equipment is on hand.

In a similar vein, when addressing enough people to merit a sound system, specify in advance (a) whether you prefer a podium microphone or a wireless clip-on, (b) if you need microphones for audience questions, and (c) whether or not they have backup systems in place should any of the front-line microphones fail to work properly.

Backup Plan

In short: have one, especially when using PowerPoint. If you are bringing a presentation on your laptop, have a copy on a CD or portable drive with you as well. If you sent your presentation in advance, it is still worth carrying an extra copy in case the presentation was corrupted in the transfer or if there are any compatibility issues with the meeting site's equipment.

And in the event of total technological meltdown, be prepared to proceed without any visual support. Just remember: The audience is coming to see you, not your slides, and when a light bulb suddenly burns out or a computer abruptly crashes, the show must go on!

Let There Be Lumens!
The Lowdown on LCD Projectors

After spending all those hours designing your PowerPoint presentation, you want clear, crisp images on the screen come showtime. Even when room lights remain on or natural daylight streams in from outside, a powerful projector can deliver the sharp images you desire.

For LCD projectors, power is measured in lumens (i.e., light output). The typical portable projector that most nonprofits own puts out around 1,200 lumens, which is suitable for an audience of 30 to 40 people. When you are speaking to an audience of 100 or more, however, you need a projector with a minimum of 2,500 lumens and at least one screen that is 10 feet wide by 10 feet tall.

Venues such as hotels and conference centers often have projectors with even more lumens, and they will usually have dual projector-and-screen setups in rooms designed for large audiences. It is not unusual, however, to encounter situations where a host nonprofit has brought its own low-end portable into a large hotel ballroom "... because the projector rental fee was *outrageous*!" Don't leave this detail to chance: Before you arrive on the scene, talk to your event organizer and make sure you have the right amount of lumens working for you.

How You Are Introduced

In *The Toastmasters International Guide to Successful Speaking*, co-authors Jeff Slutsky and Michael Aun write, "Your introduction is the beginning of your beginning. It should not be a separate element that is out of your control." And given that the first few seconds of your talk are critical in winning over the audience, the last thing you want to do is spend that time recovering from what the previous speaker just said about you.

So spend a few minutes writing a standard 30-second introduction that can be read verbatim or quickly tailored to any new setting. That small investment of time can save you the trouble of having to correct the pronunciation of your name, provide your real title, or disavow any of the myriad things that introducers can (and often will) get wrong.

Handouts

The length, complexity, and production quality of handouts are generally dependent on the presentations they accompany, as well as the amount of time (and money) the presenter has to prepare them. It is difficult to offer useful advice on this topic without knowing more about the particulars of your situation. Difficult, but not impossible, because there is one aspect of handouts that is universal, and that is what audiences will do with them.

Give someone a handout and he will read it – if not the moment he gets it, the first moment he is bored with your talk. Even if you explicitly state, "You won't need to review this chart for another hour," I can guarantee the recipients are not hearing your instructions because they are already studying the chart. It's just human nature, and that's not something you are going to change.

So whenever possible, distribute handouts at the *end* of your talk, and design them to serve as a summary of the major points. This timing helps keep the audience's focus on you and provides them with one less potential distraction. If the audience must refer to handouts in the course of your presentation, distribute them as close to that moment as you can. And when event organizers from The Bizarro World insist you send all handouts in advance so they can incorporate them into conference notebooks, just say, "That's okay, I'll distribute them myself." You may ruffle some feathers, but you will be better serving your audience, and that should always be your bottom line.

Preparing for Panels

As event organizers put together conferences, they often seem to view panels as fill-in-the-blanks exercises. Pick a subject, find three experts with (hopefully) some differing views, and select a moderator to keep the train on the tracks. More experienced organizers will also arrange for the moderator and panelists to talk in advance and jointly plan the session, but it is not unusual for a panelist to enter a meeting room knowing only the names of the session and the other people on the stage.

"My standard handout is built around the idea that if I never see these people again, here are the 10 most important things they need to change the way they work."

– Dynell Garron
The Funder's Checklist

Kristen Grimm, who speaks on numerous panels in the course of a year, does not leave the preparation to chance. "I always talk to the other panelists to make sure I won't be duplicating their content," she says. When Andy Lipkis of TreePeople was asked to submit an abstract of his remarks for an upcoming panel appearance, he pushed back. "I can't give you an abstract until I know where you are going and what you want," Lipkis told the event organizers.

Many other expert commentators echoed these thoughts. At larger conferences with many breakout sessions, panels are often the planners' neglected stepchildren. Experienced presenters, however, will take matters into their own hands and arrange the necessary conference calls to ensure a sufficient level of preparation.

One other common problem afflicting this kind of presentation can best be described as "The Panelist Who Ate My Time." Thanks to the long-winded gentleman to your left, those 15 minutes for which you prepared so carefully have been cut to five, and the moderator is ever-so-nicely asking you to keep it brief and help get the session back on schedule. What do you do?

Under these circumstances, Cliff Atkinson's story template can be a very useful tool. As you can see below, the middle section of the template (Act II of the story) is divided into three columns. This allows users to enter different amounts of detail depending on the length of the story they plan on telling (5, 15, or 45 minutes). Following this same model, you could prepare for a panel by mapping out the key points you would want to make given different time limits. Now when your 15-minute window suddenly collapses to five, instead of hastily crossing out and rearranging your notes, you can simply shift your focus from one column to another and make the most of the time you have.

Use these sections to plan your remarks for panels.

Insert story title and byline here		
Act I: Set up the story		
The setting		
The protagonist		
The imbalance		
The balance		
The solution		
Act II: Develop the action		
5-Minute Column:	15-Minute Column:	45-Minute Column:
Turning point		
Act III: Frame the resolution		
The crisis		
The solution		
The climax		
The resolution		

EVALUATIONS

Nothing improves performance like measurement, and evaluation forms are the most common yardstick for presenters. Many organizations that invite you to speak will provide evaluation forms for the audience, and in those cases, it's up to you to contact the organizers after the event and ask for a copy of the results. (In my travels, I have never encountered a conference organizer who refused to share them, and in many cases they were provided before I had even asked for them.)

When meeting planners have not covered this base – a question worth adding to your pre-presentation checklist – bring your own evaluation form. (As above, I have never encountered anyone who objected to this practice.) Audiences are notoriously impatient with long questionnaires, especially when they have to dash off to another session, so keep it short. In his book, *Life is a Series of Presentations*, Tony Jeary says evaluation forms should take a maximum of three to five minutes to complete. While brevity is your watchword, though, be sure to cover the basic categories:

Category	Sample Language for Evaluation Form
CLARITY	Was the material presented in a clear and well-structured manner?
RELEVANCE	Do you see ways to use the information presented in your work?
LENGTH	Was the time allotted sufficient for the material covered?
INTERACTION WITH PRESENTER	Did you have sufficient time to interact with the presenter?
INTERACTION WITH AUDIENCE	Did you have sufficient time to interact with other members of the audience?
QUALITY OF VISUALS	How would you rate the quality of any supporting visuals (e.g., PowerPoint)?
QUALITY OF HANDOUTS	How would you rate the quality of any handouts?
PLATFORM SKILLS	Was the presenter effective in engaging the audience and making the subject matter compelling?

See **Checklists to Go**
for a detachable
summary of this section.

Sugar and Caffeine:
Your Two New Best Friends

"For an all-day session, I give specific instructions about food. I always insist that coffee is available all day long, and Coke and Diet Coke. And I always try to get people – especially when they're on a budget – not to do dessert at lunch, but to take that money and do cookies at 1:30. Getting through that "siesta" period can be a challenge. Cookies and soft drinks at 1:30 will keep 'em going 'til 3."

– CHUCK LORING
LORING, STERNBERG
& ASSOCIATES

Provide respondents with multiple-choice answers that can be quickly circled, and also include an open-ended question (e.g., "How could this presentation be improved?") that will allow them to offer any feedback not covered by your questions.

Jeary has one other piece of excellent advice: Distribute the evaluation forms at the *beginning* of your session. It reinforces the message that you are interested in your audience's opinions, conditions audience members to think critically about your presentation, and prepares them to spend a few minutes at the end writing down their thoughts. It also doesn't hurt for the audience to see you as confident enough to ask for their assessment of your work.

Before Malcolm Gladwell wrote the book, *The Tipping Point*, he introduced the concept in an essay in *The New Yorker*. In that piece, Gladwell explained how the New York City Police Department cracked down on crime by attacking its precursors, snuffing out minor criminal activity before it "tipped" into something more serious. One of the more memorable examples he offered was the police department's reaction to graffiti.

When New York cops saw graffiti popping up in a neighborhood – a reliable sign of a gang marking its territory – they promptly had it painted over. If taggers returned the next night, the cops had the painters out again the following morning. So it went until the message sunk in: Not even the smallest infraction would be tolerated. And thanks to this and similar tactics, crime went down.

To my mind, bad presentations may be our sector's version of a tipping point. Unlike graffiti, though, they are warning signs that are largely being ignored. From what I can see, we are accepting them as a fact of life, and that complacency implicitly sends a message that mediocre communications are acceptable. Low expectations become the norm, and with no real incentive to improve, presentation quality will continue the inevitable slide downward.

"I think there is nothing worse than boring presentations," says Geoffrey Canada. "I think it's a disservice to the audience and the presenter. If you have gone to all the trouble of preparing, then it's important for you to think about how you can make sure that people aren't going to sleep. You need to think about how to make your information [feel] fresh and come alive for the audience. I think we owe our audience respect, to give them a presentation that is solid, good and interesting."

As a presenter, you can use this book to answer Canada's call, and we hope you will. Keep in mind, though, that just as books about golf cannot lower your scores and those about cooking do not automatically produce gourmet meals, this book, by itself, will not make you a better presenter. You have to take the tools described here and put them to work, adapting them to your personal style as you go, and perhaps even inventing some new tools along the way. In short: *You have to get out there and do it.* All we have done so far is point you in the right direction.

But even if your place in presentations is most often in the audience, you still have a role to play. Cause Communications and I hope that you will help raise the bar for public interest presentations in whatever ways you can. If you supervise people who present, set higher standards (starting with a "no reading the slides" policy). When evaluation forms are offered, take a few minutes to complete them and offer specific feedback on what worked and what did not. And if you attend a conference with consistently sub-par sessions, pull the conference organizer aside and officially register your displeasure.

Bad presentations waste time. Your work is too important and your time is far too valuable to let that continue. Chances are, there is already another presentation on your calendar. Whether that puts you behind the podium or in the audience, consider it your first opportunity to start fresh and put what you learned here into practice.

We can do better. We certainly should expect better. Let's get started.

Resources
Recommended Reading

If you are interested in learning more about presenting on your own – from platform skills to PowerPoint and everything in between – I encourage you to consider some of the books below that contributed to our research. (All publications listed alphabetically by author.)

Beyond Bullet Points
Cliff Atkinson (Microsoft Press © 2005)

If you thought that PowerPoint presentations with bullets were as inevitable as death and taxes (and just as much fun), Cliff Atkinson has good news for you in this recently published book. PowerPoint can be used to tell stories, and Atkinson has created a template along with step-by-step instructions to help you do the same – and without those deadly bullets.

Lend Me Your Ears: All You Need to Know About Making Speeches and Presentations
Max Atkinson (Vermillion © 2004)

There's a reason Max Atkinson is quoted extensively in *Why Bad Presentations Happen to Good Causes*: He has incisive things to say about every aspect of presenting, from platform skills to visual aids to even the finest details of word choice. His popularity in North America has yet to equal that in the United Kingdom, but with the recent publication of this book in the U.S., that is certain to change soon.

Really Bad PowerPoint and How to Avoid It
Seth Godin (e-booklet)

Short, biting and filled with very specific advice, Godin's e-book can be a bit prescriptive, but at $1.99 (to download from various sources on the web) you cannot go too far wrong with this fast, entertaining read.

Multimedia Learning
Richard E. Mayer (Cambridge University Press © 2001)

With chapter titles such as "Spatial Contiguity Principle" and "Temporal Contiguity Principle," Mayer's book is the kind you would probably pull off the shelf, flip through briefly, and promptly put back. For users of PowerPoint, however, it's worth another look because Mayer speaks directly to such common questions as "How much text on a slide is too much?" and "When is it better to say it or show it?" Yes, you'll have to sift through some pretty murky passages, but valuable nuggets await the persevering reader.

Before & After Page Design
John McWade (Peachpit Press © 2003)

McWade's book is ideal for amateurs like me who must dabble in the field of graphic design – especially when laying out PowerPoint slides. The chapter with a step-by-step illustration of how to design a multiple-panel brochure from a single, cleverly folded sheet of paper (see pp. 54–63) exemplifies McWade's belief that smart design can be economical as well. *The Non-Designer's Design Book* by Robin Williams (also from Peachpit Press) covers similar territory, but if you feel sufficiently grounded in the fundamentals, *Before & After* can take you to the next level.

On Speaking Well
Peggy Noonan (Regan Books © 1999)

As a speechwriter for former Presidents Reagan and Bush, Peggy Noonan may have written the words that made you throw a shoe at your television (perhaps even a closetful of shoes), but the Washington veteran clearly knows her stuff. Her book is filled with practical advice on trimming a speech to the best length (20 minutes), ingratiating yourself with an audience (show 'em you know 'em), handling Q&A (keep it moving) and more.

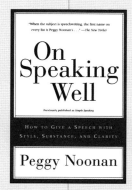

The Cognitive Style of PowerPoint
Edward Tufte (Graphic Press LLC © 2003)

Incensed that Microsoft is homogenizing presentations in elementary schools, Fortune 500 companies, and just about everywhere in between, Tufte pulls no punches in this scathing monograph. Of PowerPoint's Auto Content Wizard, he writes, "With their strict generic formats, these designer stylesheets serve only to reinforce the limitations of PowerPoint, compromising the presenter, the content, and ultimately, the audience." And that's just for starters. Tufte's report, a bargain at $7 (plus shipping) can be ordered at www.edwardtufte.com.

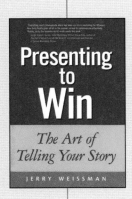

Presenting to Win – The Art of Telling Your Story
Jerry Weissman (FT Prentice Hall © 2003)

Having coached executives at Yahoo, Intel, Cisco, Microsoft and hundreds of other companies, Weissman is able to offer numerous examples of what works and what bombs based on his considerable experience in the field. The writing will not win any literary prizes, but *Presenting to Win* is filled with more than enough tips and guidelines to justify the investment.

CHECKLISTS TO GO

QUESTIONS FOR AUDIENCE RESEARCH

(see pp. 19–21 for more background)

1. Who will be in the audience?

2. What do they know or believe that I can build on?

3. What do they know or believe that I have to overcome?

4. By the end of my presentation, what do I want them to have learned?

5. By the end of my presentation, what do I want them to feel?

6. By the end of my presentation, what do I want them to do?

LOGISTICS: CONFIRM THESE DETAILS WHEN PLANNING FOR YOUR PRESENTATION

(see pp. 65–70 for more background)

1. Room setup

Decide which configuration best suits the needs of your presentation:

- classroom style: long, narrow rectangular tables facing forward
- round tables: known as "rounds," which help facilitate small group discussions
- theatre style: all seats face forward, no tables

2. Light and sound

- Projector: if you are using PowerPoint, make sure the LCD projector has sufficient illuminating power to project clear, sharp images on the screen. Projector power is measured in lumens: For an audience of 50 or fewer, 1000–2000 lumens are usually sufficient.
- Microphones: Request a wireless lapel microphone if you want to be able to roam from the podium. If you intend to take questions from an audience of more than 50 people, it is helpful to have one or two wireless microphones that can be passed around.

3. How you are introduced

Write a standard 30-second introduction that can be read verbatim or quickly tailored to any new setting in the event an introduction has not been prepared.

4. Evaluations

Ask the meeting or conference organizer if evaluation forms will be made available for participants, and if not, seek permission to bring your own.

5. Backup plan

If you are bringing a PowerPoint presentation on your laptop, have a copy on a CD or portable drive with you when you arrive for your session.

THE STRUCTURE FOR EFFECTIVE PRESENTING

(see Chapter 2 for more background)

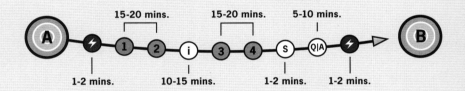

SAMPLE ONE-HOUR SESSION

RELIABLE TECHNIQUES FOR OPENING A PRESENTATION

(see pp. 32–33 for more background)

1. Telling a story that crystallizes the subject matter of your talk.

2. Asking questions that make audience members consider their personal relationship to your subject (e.g., When was the last time you sat through a truly awful presentation?).

3. Throwing out a compelling statistic (e.g., there are three times as many places to buy guns in America as there are McDonald's).

4. Showing a picture that genuinely lives up to the "thousand words" promise.

7 Questions to Sharpen Your Storytelling

(see pp. 28–29 for more background)

1. Who's the protagonist?

2. What's the hook?

3. What keeps it interesting?

4. Where's the conflict?

5. Have you included telling details?

6. What's the *emotional* hook?

7. Is the meaning clear?

7 Techniques for Using PowerPoint More Effectively

(see Chapter 4 for more background)

1. First, accept what PowerPoint is not (i.e., design a presentation to provide visual support, not to duplicate spoken content and to serve as a handout).

2. Say the words. Show the pictures.

3. Design outside the white box.

4. Use style to convey substance (e.g., your organizational identity) and structure (to help audience members visually track progress through long or complex presentations).

5. Use animation to control the flow of information and convey meaning.

6. Unify elements to create a visual hierarchy.

7. Discover the little miracles: The B key allows you to black out the screen (returning audience attention to the presenter); typing the number of a slide followed by ENTER allows you to access any slide at any time.

EVALUATION FORMS

(see pp. 69–70 for more background)

When meeting organizers have not covered this base, bring evaluation forms and distribute them prior to your presentation. To create a form for your presentation, consider the question categories and sample language below:

Category	Sample Language for Evaluation Form
CLARITY	Was the material presented in a clear and well-structured manner?
RELEVANCE	Do you see ways to use the information presented in your work?
LENGTH	Was the time allotted sufficient for the material covered?
INTERACTION WITH PRESENTER	Did you have sufficient time to interact with the presenter?
INTERACTION WITH AUDIENCE	Did you have sufficient time to interact with other members of the audience?
QUALITY OF VISUALS	How would you rate the quality of any supporting visuals (e.g., PowerPoint)?
QUALITY OF HANDOUTS	How would you rate the quality of any handouts?
PLATFORM SKILLS	Was the presenter effective in engaging the audience and making the subject matter compelling?

SURVEY DESIGN

The survey was posted on Edge Research's web site on January 5, 2005. It contained 43 questions mostly in the closed-ended format, as well as open-ended questions that would give respondents greater latitude with their feedback. Questions ranged from the very specific (e.g., "How long is the average presentation you attend?") to the more subjective (e.g., "How often do you think you learn something valuable?").

As noted earlier, respondents were asked not only to evaluate presentations they had attended, but those they had given as well. Most of the questions asked about presentations observed were repeated in the section on presentations given. Finally, we asked respondents to list the names of the best speakers they had seen, which helped us find some of the experts who contributed their insights and recommendations to this book.

RESPONDENTS

To drive qualified respondents (i.e., full-time employees of nonprofits, foundations, government agencies or educational institutions) to the web to complete the questionnaire, Cause Communications and I contacted dozens of organizations that regularly communicate with this audience. We asked for their help publicizing the online survey, and just about everyone we spoke with was willing to pitch in.

Statewide nonprofit associations in California, Florida, New York, and elsewhere sent e-mail alerts to their affiliates or ran items in newsletters. The 10 foundations that funded this book were among the nearly 30 philanthropies that used their networks to alert colleagues, grantees, and others. And too many friends to name here helped get our message out via listservs that reached thousands in the public interest community.

In just three months, this outreach generated 2,501 completed surveys. Respondents came from all over the U.S.

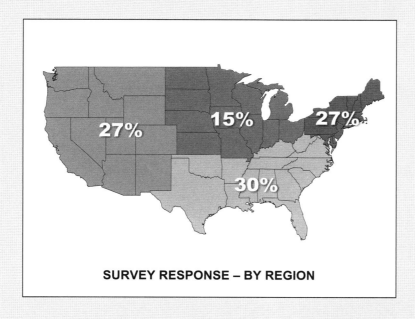

SURVEY RESPONSE – BY REGION

APPENDIX
Survey Methodology and Results – CONT'D

Respondents also represented a wide range of issues:

Children/Youth	42%	Civil Rights	10%
Health	40%	Women's Rights	9%
Education	37%	Humanitarian Aid	6%
Environment	31%	Gay & Lesbian Rights	6%
Social Justice	21%	Reproductive Rights	4%
Poverty	19%	Election Reform	3%
Housing	18%	Gun Control	1%
Employment	11%	Other	3%

Total percentage exceeds 100 since respondents were asked to check all categories that applied to their work.

We were also pleased to note that these respondents were very familiar with presentations from both sides of the podium: 76% attended presentations once a month or more, and approximately half gave a presentation just as frequently.

Since respondents to this survey were self-selecting, we cannot claim that our results are a scientifically accurate sampling of the sector. Given the sheer volume of responses, however, along with a reasonably even geographic distribution and wide coverage of issue areas, we believe the results that follow offer valuable insights regarding what works, what doesn't, and why in public interest presentations.

SECTION 1: ORGANIZATIONAL INFORMATION

1. In which of the following sectors do you work:

   Foundation......................................11%
   Nonprofit 71
   Government.......................................7
   Association 2
   Other...9

2. Which of the following best describes your current employment status?

   Full-time 86%
   Part-time...6
   Board member..................................2
   Not currently employed..................1
   Full-time student 1
   Retired 2
   Other...2

3. On what issue areas do you work? [Multiple responses accepted] (n=2062)

   Children/Youth..............................42%
   Civil Rights 10
   Gay & Lesbian Rights......................6
   Gun Control......................................1
   Education 37
   Election Reform...............................3
   Employment 11
   Environment...................................30
   Health..40
   Housing..18
   Humanitarian Aid 6
   Poverty...18
   Reproductive Rights 5
   Social Justice...................................21
   Women's Rights................................9
   Other...3

4. How many employees work in your organization?

   1–25 ....49%
   26–250 30
   Over 250 19
   Don't know 2

5. What would you estimate your organization's annual operating budget to be?

   Less than $1 million 32%
   $1–10 million..................................37
   Over $10 million.............................24
   Don't know/Refused 7

6. Approximately how many years have you worked in this sector?

   1–5...37%
   6–10 25
   11–20...22
   21 + ...16

APPENDIX
Survey Methodology and Results – CONT'D

SECTION 2: EVALUATING OTHERS

The purpose of this section is to learn more about your experiences watching presentations. For the purposes of this survey, a "presentation" is defined as any situation in which a speaker has been asked in advance to prepare a talk on a specific subject for a specific audience.

7. About how often do you think you *attend* presentations?

    More than once a week 7%
    About once a week 14
    A few times a month...................... 36
    Once a month............................... 19
    A few times a year 22
    Once a year 1
    Less than once a year 1
    Don't know ....*

8. How long is the average presentation you attend?

    5–10 minutes. 2%
    10–20 minutes................................. 19
    20–40 minutes 33
    40–60 minutes. 26
    1 hr. or more 18

9. How often do these presentations use supporting visuals, such as PowerPoint, slides, or charts? (1=never, 5=always)

    Never–1 .... 1%
    2.. 10
    3.. 27
    4.. 45
    Always–5 17
    Don't know ....*

10. How would you rate the quality of these visuals? (1=poor, 5=excellent)

    Poor–1... 5%
    2.. 24
    3.. 51
    4.. 18
    Excellent–5.................................... 2
    Don't know 1

11. How often do these presentations use hand-outs, leave-behinds, or other printed materials distributed to attendees? (1=never, 5=always)

    Never–1 .... 1%
    2.. 13
    3.. 26
    4.. 41
    Always–5 19
    Don't know 1

12. How would you rate the quality of these materials? (1=poor, 5=excellent)

    Poor–1... 3%
    2.. 19
    3.. 52
    4.. 22
    Excellent–5.................................... 2
    Don't know 2

13. During a typical presentation you attend, how often are you or other audience members asked to interact with the speaker (not including Q&A)? (1=never, 5=always)

    Never–1 .... 8%
    2.. 42
    3.. 27
    4.. 18
    Always–5 6
    Don't know ....*

14. During a typical presentation you attend, how often are you asked to interact with other members of the audience? (1=never, 5=always)

Never–1 .... 26%
2 47
3 19
4 6
Always–5 2
Don't know .... *

15. How often do you think you learn something valuable from these presentations? (1=never, 5=always)

Never–1 .... 1%
2 14
3 51
4 30
Always–5 4
Don't know .... *

16. How would you rate the typical presentation you attend? (1=poor, 5=excellent)

Poor–1 .... 2%
2 20
3 60
4 17
Excellent–5 1
Don't know .... *

Open-ended

Verbatim responses to open-ended question are not included here due to space limitations.

17. Think back to the last excellent presentation you attended. What one or two key things make a presentation "excellent"?

_____

_____

_____

18. What one or two key things make a presentation "poor"?

_____

_____

_____

19. When was the last time you sat through a really **excellent** presentation?

Within the last week 6%
Within the last month 19
Within the last six months............ 41
Within the last year 19
More than a year ago 11
Don't know 4

20. When was the last time you sat through a really **poor** presentation?

Within the last week 17%
Within the last month 37
Within the last six months............ 32
Within the last year 8
More than a year ago 3
Don't know 2

APPENDIX
Survey Methodology and Results – CONT'D

21. Below is a list of problems that can affect presentations. Please rank each problem to indicate both how *frequently* you observe it (1=never, 5=always) and how harmful that problem is to the overall presentation. (1=not harmful at all, 5=extremely harmful).

PROBLEM

How Frequent?
(Questions in this battery were automatically rotated.)

	Never 1	2	3	4	Always 5	Don't know
The overall objective of the talk was not clear to the audience.	9%	41	36	13	1	1
The objective was not made *relevant* to the audience's concerns.	4%	34	41	18	1	2
The presentation ran too long.	2%	20	38	35	5	*
Sufficient time was not allotted for the presenter to cover all the material.	6%	31	35	24	3	1
Time was not allocated to ask questions or engage the presenter in a discussion.	7%	29	36	26	2	*
The material was poorly organized.	3%	36	44	15	1	*
The amount of material presented was overwhelming.	6%	35	37	21	2	*
There was not enough information to help the audience make a decision or reach a conclusion.	8%	38	36	13	1	4
The material was overly complex.	12%	46	30	10	1	1
Translating the material into PowerPoint templates (e.g., bullet lists) made it more difficult to understand, less interesting, or both.	14%	32	27	20	5	3
The speaker did not connect with the audience.	2%	26	48	22	1	*
The speaker was too nervous.	11%	55	27	4	*	1
The speaker was not well prepared.	7%	52	33	7	1	*
The presentation duplicated the content of the slides and/or handouts without adding anything significant.	3%	13	28	48	7	1
Technical problems (e.g., poor sound system, malfunctioning projector) disrupted the presentation.	6%	46	31	16	1	1
The presentation was not tailored to the size of the audience.	10%	42	33	10	1	4

How Harmful?

	Not harmful at all 1	2	3	4	Extremely harmful 5	Don't know
The overall objective of the talk was not clear to the audience.	3%	7	20	36	32	2
The objective was not made *relevant* to the audience's concerns.	2%	6	19	35	35	3
The presentation ran too long.	3%	14	28	35	19	1
Sufficient time was not allotted for the presenter to cover all the material.	4%	15	35	32	11	2
Time was not allocated to ask questions or engage the presenter in a discussion.	4%	13	28	35	18	2
The material was poorly organized.	2%	6	20	40	31	1
The amount of material presented was overwhelming.	4%	14	30	33	17	2
There was not enough information to help the audience make a decision or reach a conclusion.	3%	12	32	32	14	7
The material was overly complex.	6%	13	28	32	18	3
Translating the material into PowerPoint templates (e.g., bullet lists) made it more difficult to understand, less interesting, or both.	12%	20	28	22	12	5
The speaker did not connect with the audience.	1%	5	18	36	39	1
The speaker was too nervous.	9%	27	33	20	8	3
The speaker was not well prepared.	2%	6	11	29	51	2
The presentation duplicated the content of the slides and/or handouts without adding anything significant.	5%	14	27	30	22	2
Technical problems (e.g., poor sound system, malfunctioning projector) disrupted the presentation.	4%	18	27	29	20	2
The presentation was not tailored to the size of the audience.	6%	20	37	23	8	7

OPEN-ENDED

Verbatim responses to open-ended question are not included here due to space limitations.

22. Other problems not listed here?

———————————————————

———————————————————

———————————————————

23. Who were the best presenters you have seen in the past year or two? (Please list their names, affiliations (if you recall), and the subject of their presentations.)

———————————————————

———————————————————

———————————————————

Section 3: Self Evaluation

The purpose of this section is to learn more about your experience *giving* presentations. As in the previous section, a "presentation" is still defined as any situation in which you have been asked in advance to prepare a talk on a specific subject for a specific audience.

24. About how often do you **give** presentations?

More than once a week .... 4 %
Once a week... 5
A few times a month............................ 21
Once a month... 17
A few times a year 40
Once a year 4
Less than once a year 5
Don't give presentations 5
Don't know .... *

25. How long is the average presentation you give? (n=2374)

5–10 minutes .... 14 %
10–20 minutes.......................................38
20–40 minutes.......................................27
40–60 minutes 14
1 hr. or more 8

26. What is the size of the typical group to which you will present? (n=2374)

1–5 .... 3 %
6–10 11
11–20..36
21–50..41
51–100 7
100 + ... 2

27. How much time, on average, do you spend preparing for a presentation? (n=2374)

None.. *
30 mins. or less ....8 %
30 mins.–1 hr. 17
1–2 hrs. 28
More than 2 hrs. 47

28. How often do you rehearse for a presentation, either alone or for a test audience? (1=never, 5=always) (n=2374)

Never–1 .... 11 %
2...24
3...20
4... 19
Always–5...26
Don't know .... *

29. When you are asked to give a presentation, how often do you feel you have been properly briefed on the audience and their expectations of what you will talk about? (1=never, 5=always) (n=2374)

Never–1 .... 3 %
2...18
3...31
4...33
Always–5...14
Don't know 1

APPENDIX
Survey Methodology and Results – CONT'D

30. How often do your presentations use supporting visuals, such as PowerPoint, slides, or charts? (1=never, 5=always) (n=2374)

   Never–1 .... 7 %
   2 17
   3 22
   4 26
   Always–5 27
   Don't know .... *

31. How would you rate the quality of these visuals? (1=poor, 5=excellent) (n=2374)

   Poor–1 .... 2 %
   2 8
   3 35
   4 37
   Excellent–5 10
   Don't know 9

32. How often do your presentations use handouts, leave-behinds, or other printed materials distributed to attendees?
(1=never, 5=always) (n=2374)

   Never–1 .... 2 %
   2 10
   3 17
   4 29
   Always–5 42
   Don't know .... *

33. How would you rate the quality of these materials? (1=poor, 5=excellent)
(n=2374)

   Poor–1 .... *
   2 .... 4 %
   3 29
   4 48
   Excellent–5 16
   Don't know 3

34. Within a typical presentation, how often do you interact with members of the audience (<u>not</u> including Q&A)? (1=never, 5=constantly) (n=2374)

   Never–1 .... 2 %
   2 11
   3 23
   4 36
   Constantly–5 27
   Don't know .... *

35. Within a typical presentation, how often do you ask members of the audience to interact with each other? (1=never, 5=constantly) (n=2374)

   Never–1 .... 22 %
   2 28
   3 25
   4 18
   Constantly–5 6
   Don't know 1

36. How much formal training have you had to improve your presentation skills? (1=none, 3=some, 5= significant amount) (n=2374)

   None–1 .... 25 %
   2 19
   Some–3 34
   4 12
   Significant amount–5 10
   Don't know .... *

   If some or more, please describe or list titles of workshops attended.

   _____

   _____

   _____

37. How many publications have you read to help improve your presentation skills? (1=none, 3=some, 5= significant amount) (n=2374)

None–1..25 %
2...26
Some–3..33
4...9
Significant amount–5...........................6
Don't know 1

If some or more, please list titles of publications or articles.

_____

_____

_____

38. How often do you seek and/or get feedback on your presentations (through a formal evaluation process, contacting one or more presentation attendees, etc.)? (1=never, 5=always) (n=2374)

Never–1 ....12 %
2...20
3...22
4...23
Always–5...23
Don't know ....*

39. Overall, how would you rate yourself as a presenter? (1=poor, 3=average, 5=excellent) (n=2374)

Poor–1...1 %
2...6
Average–3..43
4...41
Excellent–5 8
Don't know 1

40. Overall, how would you describe your feelings when you are asked to present to an audience? (1=dread it, 5=look forward to it) (n=2374)

Dread–1...7 %
2...12
3...25
4...24
Look forward to it–5...........................32
Don't know ....*

Open-ended

Verbatim responses to open-ended question are not included here due to space limitations.

41. As a presenter yourself, where do you see the most room for improvement?

_____

_____

_____

(Questions 42–43 pertained to survey follow-up.)

APPENDIX
Meet the Experts

Cause Communications and I would once again like to acknowledge and thank the following individuals who generously shared their time and expertise with us. We encourage readers to visit their websites and to consider these speakers for future meetings.

Cliff Atkinson, President, Sociable Media (Los Angeles, CA)
A writer, keynote speaker, and independent management consultant to top Fortune 500 companies, Atkinson founded Sociable Media in 2001 to help clients use media in more engaging ways. His proficiency with PowerPoint led Microsoft to invite him to write *Beyond Bullet Points* (which the company published under its own banner in 2005). Atkinson has been invited to speak at the Wharton School of Business at the University of Pennsylvania, the Anderson School of Management at UCLA, and for numerous corporate clients. *www.sociablemedia.com*

Max Atkinson, President, Atkinson Communications (Wells, Somerset, U.K.)
A consultant on presentation skills, public speaking, speech writing and speaker training, Max (no relation to Cliff) has worked for numerous companies in the UK and beyond. In 1985, he ran a seminar on speech writing in the Reagan White House. His book, *Lend Me Your Ears: All You Need to Know About Making Speeches and Presentations* (Random House UK, 2004) was published in the U.S. in the fall of 2005. *www.speaking.co.uk*

Joel Bradshaw, President, Joel Bradshaw Associates (Falls Church, VA)
A veteran political consultant and speaker, Bradshaw has worked on over 300 campaigns at all levels, including the successful U.S. Senate bids of Barbara Boxer (D-CA) and Patty Murray (D-WA). He has authored campaign manuals for the Democratic Congressional Campaign Committee, the Democratic Senatorial Campaign Committee, as well as the American Medical Association. Bradshaw speaks about strategic planning, political strategy and message development, conducting as many as 100 presentations in a single year. *orderoutofchaos@aol.com*

Geoffrey Canada, President & CEO, Harlem Children's Zone (New York, NY)
Author of *Fist Stick Knife Gun: A Personal History of Violence in America*, Canada was the recipient of the first Heinz Award in 1994 for his work at Harlem Children's Zone (HCZ), which he joined in 1983. (HCZ works to enhance the quality of life for children and families in some of New York City's most devastated neighborhoods.) Canada holds a master's degree in Education from Harvard University and has received honorary degrees from Harvard University, Williams College, Wheelock College, John Jay College of Criminal Justice, the Bank Street College of Education, and Lombard Theological Seminary. *www.hcz.org*

Marc Freedman, Founder & President, Civic Ventures (San Francisco, CA)
Author of *Prime Time: How Baby Boomers Will Revolutionize Retirement and Transform America*, Freedman launched Civic Ventures to help more Americans find meaningful work in the second half of life. Freedman received the 1995 Atlantic Fellowship in Public Policy and has been a guest commentator in *The New York Times*, *The Washington Post*, *The Wall Street Journal*, and on National Public Radio. *www.civicventures.org*

Dynell Garron, Founder, The Funder's Checklist (Oakland, CA)
The former director of Gap Foundation, Garron has developed and implemented grantmaking and community relations strategies for Gap, Old Navy and Banana Republic stores across the United States. She is author of *The Funder's Checklist: An Inside Look at How Funders Evaluate Proposals and Nonprofit Organizations* and founded her company in 2002 to help nonprofits navigate the grant-seeking process more effectively. *www.funderschecklist.com*

Kristen Grimm, President, Spitfire Strategies (Washington, DC)
Grimm has extensive experience conceiving, implementing and managing strategic communications campaigns. Her company provides communications solutions to support positive social change, working with such clients as New American Dream, Open Society Institute, and The Robert Wood Johnson Foundation. In 2003, Spitfire Strategies launched the Communications Leadership Institute to train nonprofit executive directors in communications strategy and campaign tactics. Grimm is also the creator of "The Smart Chart," a widely used communication planning tool. She conducts as many as 200 presentations a year. *www.spitfirestrategies.com*

Paul Hawken, Founder, Natural Capital Institute (Sausalito, CA)
An environmentalist, entrepreneur, journalist, and best-selling author, Hawken's most recent book is *Natural Capitalism: Creating the Next Industrial Revolution* (co-authored by Amory Lovins). He has founded or co-founded several companies including Groxis, Smith & Hawken, and several of the first natural food companies in the U.S that relied solely on sustainable agricultural methods. In a busy year he will deliver as many as 60 keynote addresses. *www.paulhawken.com*

Kim Klein, Founder & Publisher, *Grassroots Fundraising Journal* (Oakland, CA)
Widely in demand as a speaker, Klein has provided training and consultation in fundraising in all 50 states as well as 19 countries around the globe. Besides publishing her monthly journal for the past 25 years, Klein currently serves as the Chardon Press Series Editor at Jossey-Bass Publishers, which publishes and distributes materials for the nonprofit sector. *www.grassrootsfundraising.org*

Christina Harbridge Law, President, Bridgeport Financial, Inc. (San Francisco, CA)
While Law's principle focus is running Bridgeport Financial, Inc., a debt collection agency, she has developed a considerable reputation as a presentation and public speaking coach for corporate and nonprofit clients. She has served as president of the California Association of Collectors, as well as a continuing education instructor for the Bar Association. In a typical year, Law will deliver approximately 20 speeches and conduct 25–30 presentation or public speaking trainings. *www.bridgeportfinancial.com*

Andy Lipkis, Founder & President, TreePeople (Beverly Hills, CA)
Lipkis founded TreePeople, an environmental organization working in Southern California, in 1974. He and his wife, Katie, co-authored the book, *The Simple Act of Planting a Tree*, and were jointly named to the United Nations Environmental Program's Global 500 Honor Roll. They also hold American Forests' Lifetime Achievement Award, and TreePeople was designated a Point of Light by President George Bush in 1991. Lipkis makes about 50 presentations a year. *www.treepeople.org*

Chuck V. Loring, CFRE, Senior Partner, Loring, Sternberg & Associates (Ft. Lauderdale, FL)
Loring, Sternberg & Associates provides fundraising and governance consulting services to nonprofits. Loring has worked with a wide variety of organizations, including Easter Seals, the Susan G. Komen Foundation, and the Alzheimer's Association. He is past president of the Indiana Chapter of the Association of Fundraising Professionals, and serves as a senior governance associate for BoardSource in Washington, DC (formerly the National Center for Nonprofit Boards). In a busy year, Loring will conduct as many as 100 presentations. *www.lsacounsel.com*

Nancy Lublin, CEO, Do Something (New York, NY)
Before joining Do Something, Lublin founded and led Dress for Success, a nonprofit organization that provides interview suits, career development training, and confidence boosts to women in more than 70 cities in four countries. During her tenure at Dress for Success, Lublin won awards from *Forbes*, *Ms. Magazine*, and *Fast Company*, and she was named Woman of the Year by the New York City Women's Commission. *www.dosomething.org*

Holly Minch, Project Director, SPIN Project (San Francisco, CA)
As part of her role in leading the SPIN Project, a nonprofit communications consulting firm, Minch directs the SPIN Academy, offering training and coaching in communications strategy and tactics to help progressive organizations become more media savvy. She is also editor of the book, *Loud and Clear in an Election Year*. In an average year, Minch leads 75–100 trainings across the U.S. *www.spinproject.org*

Lorraine Monroe, President & CEO, Lorraine Monroe Leadership Institute (New York, NY)
Dr. Monroe was the founding principal of the Frederick Douglass Academy in Central Harlem. She has drawn on her deep experience in New York City's public school system – from teacher to principal to deputy chancellor for Curriculum and Instruction – to develop leadership principles that are now taught through her institute. She is the author of *Nothing's Impossible: Leadership Lessons from Inside and Outside the Classroom*, and her work has been featured in *The New York Times, Ebony Magazine, Fast Company*, and on *60 Minutes* and *Tony Brown's Journal*. *www.lorrainemonroe.com*

Peg Neuhauser, President, PCN Associates (Austin, TX)
Neuhauser launched her management consulting firm in 1984, and now speaks widely on such topics as organizational effectiveness, avoiding burnout, and conflict resolution within organizations. She is the author of several books, including *Corporate Legends and Lore, Tribal Warfare in Organizations*, and *I Should Be Burnt Out by Now ... So How Come I'm Not?* In a typical year, she'll deliver 100 presentations. *www.pegneuhauser.com*

Eda Roth, Eda Roth & Associates (Boston, MA)
An actress and consultant who brings theatre-based skills to business communications, Roth has coached corporate clients at AT&T, Coca-Cola, and Hewlett-Packard, as well as public interest professionals at California Health Care Foundation, Robert Wood Johnson Foundation Executive Nurse Fellows Program, and the UCLA Medical School. She has been on the faculty of Boston University's School of Management Leadership Institute since 1989, and recently joined the faculty of Spitfire Strategies' Communications Leadership Institute. *www.edaroth.com*

Gerry Tabio, President, Creative Resources (Bixby, OK)
Tabio teaches a proprietary process in creative problem solving to media and marketing professionals. His client list includes America Online, National Association of Broadcasters, Turner Entertainment, and Toyota Motor Sales. Prior to launching Creative Resources, Tabio served as senior vice president of Chancellor Media Corporation. *www.gerrytabio.com*

Scott Ward, Senior Vice President, Widmeyer Communications (Washington, DC)
Ward provides training, strategy and counsel for nonprofit, business and government clients at Widmeyer Communications, a public relations firm with offices in Washington, DC and New York. He also conducts classes for nonprofit professionals at the Social Action and Leadership School for Activists (SALSA) of the Institute for Policy Studies in Washington, DC. *www.widmeyer.com*

Jerry Weissman, Founder, Power Presentations, Ltd. (Foster City, CA)
As a corporate presentations coach since 1988, Weissman has worked with executives at companies including Yahoo!, Intel, Cisco Systems, Microsoft and Dolly Labs. He is the author of *Presenting to Win: The Art of Telling Your Story* and *In the Line of Fire: How to Handle Tough Questions ... When it Counts*. *www.powerltd.com*